A YEAR
IN THE
WOODS

Paul Clements is the author of five travel books about Ireland. His writing reflects the cultural landscape, heritage and natural world. He has also written two biographies: one on the Irish writer, actor and singer Richard Hayward (2014), and the other on the Welsh travel writer and historian Jan Morris, published in 2022. A former BBC assistant editor, he is a contributor to *The Irish Times*. He lives with his wife and son in Belfast.

A YEAR IN THE WOODS

Montalto through the Seasons

PAUL CLEMENTS

MERRION
PRESS

First published in 2025 by
Merrion Press
10 George's Street
Newbridge
Co. Kildare
Ireland
www.merrionpress.ie

978 1 78537 548 4 (Paper)
978 1 78537 553 8 (eBook)

A CIP catalogue record for this book is available from the British Library.

Main text typeset in Minion Pro, 11/17

Cover design by kvaughan.com

Merrion Press is a member of Publishing Ireland.

MIX
Paper | Supporting
responsible forestry
FSC
www.fsc.org   FSC® C021394

To Felicity,

who shared my happiness in the woods.

'There can be no really black melancholy to him who lives in the midst of nature and has still his senses.'

Henry David Thoreau, *The Journal*, 1845

'It is not so much for its beauty that the forest makes a claim upon men's hearts, as for that subtle something, that quality of air, that emanation from old trees, that so wonderfully changes and renews a weary spirit.'

R.L. Stevenson, *Essays of Travel*, 1905

Contents

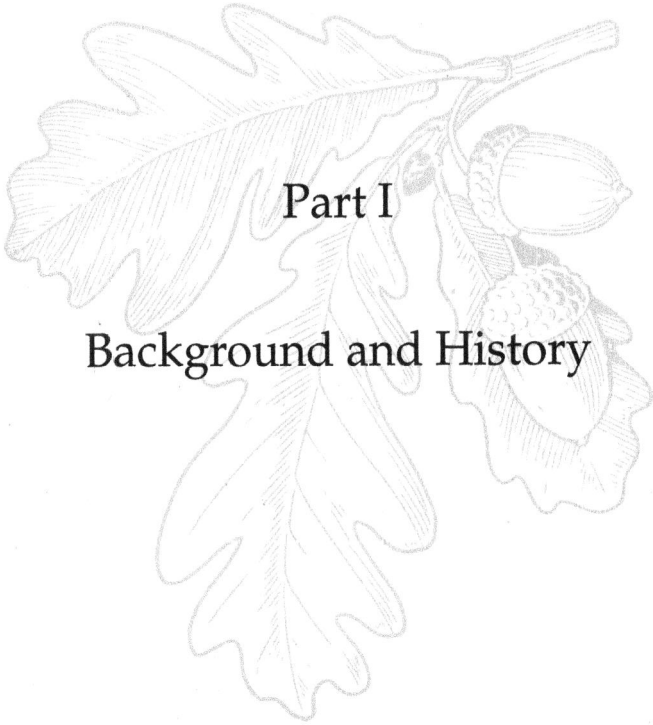

Part I

Background and History

Chronology of Montalto Estate

1641   The estate grounds are founded following the Irish rebellion, when land in the area under the control of the McCartan family is confiscated.

1653   Patrick McCartan is hanged in Carrickfergus for his involvement in the rebellion.

1657   Townland at Ballymaglave North is purchased by Sir George Rawdon, who moves from Yorkshire to Ireland.

1755–65 His great-grandson, John, Earl of Moira, a botanist, moves the family seat to Montalto.

1762–69 The decorative plasterwork ceiling and walls of the lady's sitting room are installed.

1773–93 Over a twenty-year period, improvements to the gardens at Montalto cost £30,000, while a total of 100,000 trees are planted and a pinetum created with rare specimens.

1780s   The estate opens to the public two days each week, with locals encouraged to visit.

1792   Theobald Wolfe Tone visits Montalto seeking support from Lord Moira for the United Irishmen.

1793   Death of Lord Moira; the estate passes to the 2nd earl, Francis Rawdon-Hastings.

1797   The 2nd earl removes the library to his English seat at Castle Donington in Leicestershire. A meeting is held with his tenants in Ballynahinch to calm tensions rising throughout County

Down and other parts of Ireland. A United Irish cell is discovered at Montalto and weapons are found in the demesne.

1798   During the Battle of Ballynahinch, in June, the grounds are at the centre of the United Irishmen's insurrection. Lord Moira puts up the estate for sale in September.

1802–03 The house and grounds, with 400 acres, are purchased for a knock-down price by David Guardi (D.G.) Ker.

1820   The house is redesigned by the architect William Morrison and larger windows added.

1837   D.G. Ker makes major improvements and rebuilds the house. A new ground floor is added along with a Doric porch at the front entrance.

1839   Thousands of the estate's finest trees are uprooted and destroyed during the 'Night of the Big Wind', 6 January, the Night of the Epiphany.

1844   David Stewart Ker inherits the house after his father's death.

1845–47 During the Great Famine, around 1847, the new front Doric portico is removed because paupers caused 'inconvenience' to the Ker family by sheltering under it.

1850s   D.S. Ker adds a two-storey ballroom wing to the west of the house, together with a new service area and renovation of the upstairs bedrooms.

1867–68 An arch and palazzo-style gate lodge commissioned by D.S. Ker are designed for the entrance, but neither is built.

1871–72 D.S. Ker is arrested in Sackville Street, Dublin and taken to the City Marshalsea debtors' prison. He is declared bankrupt and management of the estate is placed in the hands of trustees.

1872   Alfred Ker inherits the indebted remains of the Ker estates.

1877   Alfred Ker dies in December, aged thirty-four.

1884   Captain Richard William Blackwood Ker, the last of the Ker family to live at Montalto, is appointed High Sheriff of County Down.

1884–85 Attempts are made to auction off Montalto's art collection to raise money. Kennels in the estate are let, blood- and livestock are sold, but not enough money is raised. Bailiffs are rumoured to have been called in and seizure of the house is threatened.

1887   An intervention takes place and the estate remains solvent.

1898   The Ker family falls on hard times again with Richard Ker ending up in the bankruptcy court with the estate £89,000 in debt.

1910   Richard Ker is forced to place the estate in receivership but has difficulty finding a buyer.

1911   Richard Ker attempts to fell 700 trees in the demesne to make money but is prevented by his wife.

1912   The house is sold to Arthur Vesey Meade, 5th Earl of Clanwilliam, for £20,000.

1913   As part of Home Rule protests the grounds are used for training by Ulster Volunteers billeted in the farmyard.

1930s   Efforts are made to carry out improvements to the gardens. In 1938 the first meeting of the Ulster branch of the Alpine Gardening Society is held at Montalto when an exhibition of alpine plants is staged at a garden fete.

1939–45 American armed forces are billeted in the estate during the Second World War and it is pressed into service as a vehicle maintenance depot.

1950   Lord Clanwilliam tries to sell the house but is unable to find a buyer.

1953   John Charles Edmund, 6th Earl of Clanwilliam, inherits the property and takes up residence.

1960s   Local people continue to be employed to help with farming and working in the dairy.

1979–80 The estate is put on the market and a business consortium, John Hogg and James P. Corry & Son, combines to buy it for around £1 million.

1984   Part of the estate, covering 270 acres, along with the dairy unit and milking parlour, calving bays, calf pens, slurry tanks and silos are offered for sale.

1985   A devastating fire threatens to destroy Montalto house, but the damage is confined to part of the east wing and rear apartments.

1986–90 The business partnership abolishes farming activities and sells off livestock.

1990–93 Lakeside Cottage is leased to tenants for short-term lets and commercial events take place, logs are sold and corporate activities are held.

1994   The estate is sold as a family home to Gordon and June Wilson.

1996   The Wilson family moves in to live in the main house.

2009   The house ceases to be the Wilson family residence and opens as a private-hire venue.

2011   The estate's listed nineteenth-century threshing mill is converted as The Carriage Rooms, opening for weddings and corporate entertaining.

2014 & 2016 Battle of Ballynahinch re-enactments are held in the demesne.

2016   Filming of the Disney musical drama *The Lodge* takes place in the grounds.

2017   Storm Ophelia causes damage to the woodlands, bringing down a beech tree planted in 1801.

2018   A rejuvenated Montalto demesne, fresh with horticultural changes, opens to the public as a repurposed amenity forest and showpiece.

2024   Storm Ashley (October) and Storm Darragh (December) cause considerable damage in the grounds.

2025   The exceptionally dangerous Storm Éowyn in January causes further significant damage throughout the estate.

Rebellion in the Drumlins (1765–99)

'Long life to Lord Moira, and long may he reign,
We fought the last battle within his demesne,
May liberty and freedom thro' this nation flow,
And the tyrants did suffer for General Munroe.'

Anon, 'General Monro', *The '98 Reader*

In the middle of the seventeenth century, and in the heart of the drumlin hill country of County Down, a thatched house is shown in Ballymaglaghltra on William Petty's map, at or near the site of the present Montalto house in Ballymaglave North. The thatched property is believed to have been the home of Phelim McCartan, head of the McCartan dynasty, and later of his son, Patrick. Along with the O'Neill and Magennis families, the McCartans spent four centuries resisting invasion to their lands. During the Irish rebellion of 1641, Patrick McCartan attacked Lord Cromwell's Castle in Downpatrick. Twelve years later, retribution caught up with him when he went on trial and was hanged in Carrickfergus for his involvement in the rebellion.

Some time later, confirmation of the title to the manor was granted to the Rawdon family by Charles II, and Ballynahinch, 'the town of the island', was founded by Sir George Rawdon in 1657. Although the Rawdons did not live in Ballynahinch at that stage, they owned it, and Sir George was granted the charter for the town by Charles II in 1683. The family lived in Moira, eighteen miles to the west, where Sir George's son, Sir Arthur Rawdon (1662–1695), built Moira Castle in 1690, the year that King William defeated King James at the Battle of the Boyne. Sir Arthur's successor was Sir John (1690–1723), while his son, also called John (1720–1793), was created Earl of Moira, or Lord Moira, in 1762. He supported the townspeople of Ballynahinch, helping them prosper.

In the second half of the 1750s, Sir John Rawdon moved the family seat to Montalto, just outside the town, where, around 1760, he began building a two-storey house, making it his permanent home and a visible statement of wealth. In 1752 he had married Lady Elizabeth Hastings, who became Countess of Moira (Lady Moira). However, she loathed the north and detested Ballynahinch so much that he built her a palace in Dublin called Moira House – constructed at Usher's Quay – which she found much more socially congenial.

The name 'Montalto' may have come from the Italian for 'high mountain', since Italian plasterers were employed in the original construction. It is thought that the workers came from a hill town in Le Marche called Montalto, overlooking the Adriatic Sea. Alternatively, Charles Brett, the architectural historian, has suggested it could have been a fanciful name that 'sounded agreeably Italianate to eighteenth-century ears'. Another suggestion is that the house was originally called 'Mount Tally-ho', and that the name was corrupted to Montalto over the years.

Of the original two-storey house, only the small lady's sitting room remains unaltered, with its ceiling of high-quality plaster-work. It is thought that the earl brought in the stuccoist who had been working for him at Moira House to carry out the plaster-work. Architectural experts have noted that the ceiling which survives in the room is pre-1765 and resembles the work of Robert West, with birds, grapes, roses and arabesques in high relief. The central feature is of a fox riding a curricle (a horse-drawn open carriage) drawn by a cock. At one end of the room there is a triple niche of plasterwork.

Sporadic work was undertaken over the decades following construction, leading to a disordered exterior. The fish-shaped lake in front of the main east-facing entrance was developed during this period as part of the earl's pastoral vision. In the grounds, a deer park, regarded as a symbol of high status, was created. Deer were bred as food sources and hunted for pleasure, by stalking or on horseback with a pack of staghounds. The gardens of the house were also developed significantly.

The last quarter of the eighteenth century was an era renowned in Ireland for large-scale gardening and landscaping. For over 100 years there had been a trade in the importation of plants, with new gardening techniques reaching the country. Although on the periphery of Europe, Ireland was nonetheless connected to its neighbours as a source of novel plants for gardens or ideas about their scientific study. Sir Arthur Rawdon, the first earl's grandfather, was a 'plantaholic', who was later nicknamed 'The Father of Irish Gardening'. He set his sights on acquiring exotic species from various parts of the world, especially the Caribbean. He was a contemporary of Sir Hans Sloane, also from County Down and a botanist who influenced Rawdon's horticultural tastes. Sloane had gone to the West Indies in 1687 and informed Rawdon of the rare foreign trees, shrubs and plant life there, giving him advice about what he should acquire. After seeing Sloane's plants, the earl asked him for seeds, receiving instructions on how to grow them. Other friends and colleagues also supplied him with seeds, and his gardens at Moira Castle became adorned with ponds, canals, hanging gardens and woods.

In April 1692 Sir Arthur dispatched his gardener, James Harlow, to Jamaica to collect a range of more than 800 different species. They were packed into twenty wooden cases, each containing around fifty tropical plants, and, along with trees (totalling a cargo of over 1,000 plants), they were transported across the Atlantic. After arrival at Carrickfergus harbour on the Antrim coast, they were brought to Sir Arthur's estate at Moira. There, they were carefully transferred to the conservatory – one of the first in Ireland – and hothouses as he attempted to grow plants that would not normally be expected to tolerate the vagaries of the damp Irish climate. They included geraniums, the Indian trumpet honeysuckle with its crimson flower and ornamental yucca, or Adam's needle, with its sword-like, needle-sharp leaves. Species of trees brought over included the locust of Virginia, a hardwood; the parsley-leaved elder, *Pinus pinaster*, a medium-sized conifer; and espalier fruit trees, which were trained to grow against a wall.

Over a ten-year period, from 1684 to 1694, Sir Arthur assembled one of the most remarkable collections of living plants ever held in Ireland and was among the country's most important innovators in horticulture, assuring himself a significant place in the history of botany. He sent material and information about them to friends in England as well as to botanic gardens in Europe. While there were other active gardeners, it is believed that no other private individual in the country maintained such an enormous collection of tropical plants – apart from specialist orchid growers in the nineteenth century. Rawdon's gardening prowess and spirit of innovation are even more exceptional because they came to fruition at a time when the techniques available for plant transportation were primitive. Arthur Rawdon died on his birthday, 17 October 1695, but his spirit lived on with his grandson, John.

Little is known about the methods adopted for the cultivation at Moira of the exotic Jamaican plants, and although some initially flourished, they did not thrive as well as had been expected. By the 1720s a considerable number of the plants were in poor condition. In spite of this, some did survive and decades later were transferred to the Montalto demesne, where they were moved into a variety of locations, including hothouses and greenhouses. During the early 1770s the 1st earl had begun improving and sprucing up his new estate, which was to become renowned as one of the most elegant show gardens in the country. Although there is no catalogue or horticultural roll-call, records show that over a twenty-year period he spent £30,000 and planted 100,000 trees throughout the grounds. They included a large variety of fruit trees and a grapery, as well as a pinetum created with rare needle-tipped specimens from various parts of the world. It was, in short, a tree lover's nirvana, which would come to have 'champions' – individual trees that are exceptional examples of their species because of their size, age, rarity or historical significance. The demesne was enriched with shrubberies, temples, statues, ponds and walkways, while topiary, pergolas and gazebos added a grandiose flourish, along with a deep glen on one side.

As a mark of distinction and civilisation, trees were important to landlords and were in vogue in the late eighteenth century and early decades of the nineteenth. They were regarded as a protection of privacy and an announcement of significance, as well as of power and control. Historians believe that they trumpeted – and at the same time tactfully cloaked – wealth. They displayed status, without being vulgar, and implied long occupation, belonging and legitimacy of ownership. During the eighteenth century, trees were also an obsession with the Anglo-Irish, who may have felt residual guilt at the destruction of mighty oak forests a century earlier.

The exterior of the mansion, originally finished with ornamental stone, gave no hint of the grandeur of the interior, where the spacious entrance hall with Doric columns was decorated with family oil portraits. Hall furnishings included a long walnut-case clock, a Louis XV marquetry commode, a Régence commode and a pair of English saluting, or signal, cannon and displayed a Chippendale mahogany revolving rent table on a square pedestal with drawers. A hole in the middle of the table was used for the placing of rents from tenants.

Another feature of the house was the extensive library, which in the late seventeenth and eighteenth centuries was de rigueur for the nobility and gentry in country houses. The earl was intellectually curious and his library was said to contain an astonishing 30,000 books and manuscripts. Elegant illustrated volumes on botany and natural history, along with rare floras and plant catalogues, were among the collection. Aside from the books, there were also artefacts, telescopes, microscopes and other types of scientific apparatus 'to amuse the fancy as well as improve the mind' (Dooley and Ridgway, 2024).

Dinner guests, seated on Chippendale mahogany chairs covered in cut velvet, were served in the dining room. One visitor remarked that Lord Moira employed a French chef and ate off a silver plate but was shocked to find that the dinner table was lit by tallow, and not wax, candles.

Montalto house and lake are included on Taylor and Skinner's *Maps of the Roads of Ireland* (1777), which delineated a countryside of landowning regimes and prominent demesnes, bound up with the power and politics of the era. The maps reflect the interplay of distinctive physical settlement features and the prevalence of turnpikes, referring to a gate or turnstile that road users could pass through only after they had paid a toll. There was a demand among the gentry for maps that helped travellers, in their horse-drawn carriages, to negotiate routes. Through exquisite artisanry, scores of strip maps delineate straight stretches of main roads leading like slender tentacles from Dublin to the seats of the country's nobility and gentry. Castles, mansions, estates and farms are surrounded by trees, part of the vocabulary of symbols. In the case of Montalto, the drawing of a relatively small two-storey house and lake is surrounded by a plantation of rows of up to fifty tree symbols, equating to tens of thousands of trees. The estate is marked on the road from Antrim to Downpatrick, the latter town fifteen miles south.

Unless he was attending parliamentary duty in Dublin or London, the earl made Montalto his full-time residence, but the demesne was not just for his private pleasure. He encouraged locals to visit the grounds and kept two public days in the week – Thursday and Sunday – to show off the spectacular quality of the gardens. Among those invited were linen drapers attending Ballynahinch market, and, on Sundays, members of the parish clergy. With its rare shrubs, plants, trees and bursts of colour alongside a flowing scenery of green, a lake and lawn, the estate was akin to an elegantly cultivated botanical museum, creatively shaped and laid out with stylish walkways. The gardens brought a new awareness of the exotic flora, and since many of the eye-catching plants were unfamiliar to visitors, they were left in awe at the scale and style of the passionate work that had gone into their evolution. Locals were astounded by the tumultuous wealth of nature, by the money involved in financing the earl's obsession, and by how the sumptuous plant world at Montalto managed to survive against the ravages of the weather and time.

***

The Rawdons were County Down's leading Whigs – a term loosely applied to British and Irish politicians who supported reform of parliament and other liberal issues. In 1790 they paid ten guineas towards each of five local non-established churches, both Presbyterian and Catholic, showing unusual tolerance for an Irish aristocratic family at the time. Wealthy Protestants were part of the Established Church and the Ascendancy, while Presbyterians and Catholics were denied a range of civil and religious liberties by the Penal Laws. Although the laws were relaxed as the century wore on, the payment of tithes – notionally a tenth of one's income – to the Church of Ireland clergy remained a resented source of contention. In summer 1792 the liberal sympathies of the Rawdons rose to prominence when, on 16 August, one of the founding members of the Society of United Irishmen, Theobald Wolfe Tone, was entertained overnight at Montalto. Tone's visit was a failed attempt to persuade Lord Moira to join the Society formed in October 1791 in Belfast.

After Lord Moira's death in 1793 – the result of complications brought on by severe gout three years earlier – the 2nd earl took over the running of Montalto. He was frequently away on business, and in his absence his land agent, John Moore Johnston, looked after his interests, taking pride in the estate. Johnston went on to write a book, *Heterogenea or Medley for the Benefit of the Poor* (1803), which included information about Lord Moira and life at Montalto.

In March 1797 General Gerard Lake, General Officer Commanding the British forces in Ulster, declared martial law across the province of Ulster, leading to the arrest and imprisonment of members of the United Irishmen. Several months later, in August, and five years after Tone's visit, Lake launched a search of the outbuildings of Montalto for rebel arms. The Crown forces found pikes made in the estate's timber yard and, although the size of the cache is not known, it was clear that a United Irish cell was operating among Lord Moira's staff. A groom and a gardener, who had stored weapons for the cause in the demesne, were betrayed to the military and arrested. The groom was later dismissed.

Lord Moira was regarded as having done more than anyone to expose the misgovernment of Ireland during what was becoming a violent period. An outspoken critic of military repression in Ireland, he was also a close friend of the Prince of Wales. On 24 March 1797 the earl made a significant speech in the British House of Lords, stating that 'an humble address should be presented to the King, praying him to interpose his personal interference for the allaying of the alarming discontents then subsisting in Ireland'. Moira told his fellow peers:

> Before God and my country, I speak of what I myself have seen in Ireland, the most absurd, as well as the most disgusting, tyranny that any nation ever groaned under. I have seen troops sent, full of this prejudice – that every inhabitant of that kingdom is a rebel to the British government; the most wanton insults, the most grievous oppressions practised upon men of all ranks and conditions, in a part of the country as free of disturbance as the city of London.

At the same time, Lord Moira was increasingly aware that his tenants may be joining with the rebels and was mindful that Ballynahinch was one of the centres of disaffection. Sensing that serious trouble was brewing, he removed the library that had belonged to his father for safekeeping to their English seat, Donington Hall, a newly built mansion at Castle Donington in Leicestershire.

As a loyal citizen of King George III, the 2nd earl would not countenance any form of treason. In spring 1798 he held a meeting with his tenants at the market house in Ballynahinch to try to calm the tension that was rising throughout parts of Ireland. He stood facing them – Presbyterian, Catholic and Dissenter – reassuring them that King George loved the people of the area and cared deeply about their needs. A resolution of loyalty to the Crown was passed, in which the tenants vowed never to rise in rebellion, stating there was 'No Town so Loyal as Ballynahinch'.

However, the strength of Ballynahinch's loyalty was soon

tested. In summer 1798 the estate played a pivotal role in the Battle of Ballynahinch, part of the violent rebellion by the United Irishmen to overthrow English rule. Early on Monday 11 June, the rebels, led by their commander-in-chief, Henry Monro, a young draper from Lisburn, were preparing for a full-scale assault on Montalto and its large demesne. Insurgents began by shinning over the walls of the estate, requisitioning cattle and other stock. They swiftly established their headquarters at Ednavady Hill – also known as Montalto Heights – a short distance behind the big house and south-west of the town.

The United Irish were numerically superior to the Crown forces, with as many as 5,000 men, made up largely of Presbyterian radicals and a Catholic contingent led by Roger Magennis and known as The Defenders, who arrived at 1 p.m. the next day. The rebels came from an assortment of rural communities, the majority from north Down and the Ards peninsula. However, they lacked any formal training and were an unwieldy and ill-disciplined force. Although they did not have uniforms, quite a few wore green belts and coats, while others placed sprigs of green laurel and yellow ribbons in their buttonholes or hats. Some displayed a patriotic token, such as an Irish harp entwined with a shamrock instead of a crown, the lion and the unicorn lying in disarray, or the French cap of liberty. Messengers were dispatched to the surrounding countryside to request provisions and persuade more men to join. However, the response was disappointing and they had trouble recruiting locals, who were wary of their ability to tackle a trained army. One of a group of men from the Rathfriland area of south Down who reached Montalto was William Brunty (before later generations Brontëfied their surname by adding the diaeresis), uncle of the literary sisters Charlotte, Emily and Anne; after the battle he went into hiding.

The women of Ballynahinch were supportive of their men. Buttermilk, oatcakes and generous portions of boiled salted beef and bacon were carried by them in procession to the rebel camp. Although there was uncertainty about the scale of the forthcoming engagement, the women were conducted on a carnival-style tour of the Montalto demesne, with the United Irishmen adopting a bullish attitude to the fast-approaching denouement. Several barrels of whiskey appeared and some of the rebels became the worse for drink. The Covenanter (Reformed Presbyterian) detachment, outraged by their behaviour, left for home.

The weather was hot, with glorious sunshine, and many of the rebels lay down in the shade of the huge oaks and beeches. Scented aromas of spruce, geranium and hemlock filled the air, and they enjoyed looking at the exotic shrubs planted decades earlier. The sublime scene resembled a pleasure park, but realism intruded when the women were shown the diverse types of weapons, such as pikes and swords. Even though many may not have been aware of the scale of the coming battle, they understood that the demesne would be the cynosure of the action.

The experience of that day was recounted years later. One memory was written by James Thompson, then a boy of twelve, whose uncle was a gardener at Montalto. His father's house was at Spamount, near Ballynahinch, to which Monro's message requesting support had come. Twenty-seven years later, Thompson, who helped to carry food to the rebel encampment, captured the ambience of the event in the *Belfast Magazine* with the title 'Recollections of the Battle of Ballynahinch, by an Eyewitness':

When we arrived there were on the ground a considerable number of females, chiefly servants, or the daughters or wives of cottiers or small farmers ... Two or three young men offered their services to conduct us through the field. Everything was explained with minuteness: pikes of different constructions were pointed out and their uses explained; the cannon and ammunition were shown; the tremendous effects glanced at, which they were calculated to produce. The leaders were also pointed out – the more distinguished and greater favourites amongst them – with pride and exultation, and their dresses and ornaments explained.

In *The Summer Soldiers*, the historian A.T.Q. Stewart perceptively described the assemblage:

A kind of Sabbath sobriety broods over the scene, the familiar church outing blessed by a sunny summer day ... The business of the meeting was to sever Ireland from the dominion of Britain, to give her a separate existence and a name among the nations, to abolish tithes and taxes and give liberty and equality to all ... to make Ireland at least as happy as the United States and the French Republic were considered to be. So the men put on their best clothes, as they would for a funeral or a church service, and the women baked the cakes and brought the clean shirts, for this was the way that things were done.

On the morning of Tuesday 12 June, a lengthy column of Crown forces, made up of horse, foot and artillery, marched from

Belfast across the Long Bridge, the principal route into County Down. Under the command of Major General George Nugent, who oversaw all forces in Ulster, the expedition was more than three miles long. The military comprised soldiers from the Monaghan Regiment of Militia, known as the Monaghans, the Fifeshire Fencibles, and sixty men from the 22nd Light Dragoons, nicknamed 'Satan's bloodhounds'. Half a dozen six-pounder cannon, two howitzers and ammunition wagons were manned by the Royal Artillery. As they marched southward through fields and crossroads, the air was ominously filled with the beating of the militia drums, the skirl of the Fifeshire pipes and the pounding hoofs of the cavalry. The regiments, although not all the soldiers, had had first-hand experience of fighting just a few days earlier at the Battle of Antrim and at Saintfield, north of Ballynahinch. They had been sent orders to rendezvous in advance with other regiments, which included the York Fencibles, Hillsborough Yeomanry Cavalry and Downpatrick Yeomanry Infantry.

When they reached Ballynahinch, they dislodged a rebel outpost on Windmill Hill, to the north-west of the town, setting up their headquarters there. One of the insurgents, Hugh McCulloch, a grocer from Bangor and colonel in the United Irishmen, was captured and hanged from one of the mill's sails. Nugent issued a weighty proclamation warning that unless the rebels laid down their arms he would set fire to and destroy Killinchy, Killyleagh, Ballynahinch and Saintfield, as well as cottages and farms in the vicinity. He was true to his word, and Saintfield, along with surrounding farmhouses and haggards (hay-yards) were set on fire and burnt to the ground.

With towns being set alight, the rebel leaders were divided

about what strategy to adopt. Their military hardware was far from the awesome firepower of the Crown forces. The United Irishmen's pikes had eight-feet-long wooden shafts and sharpened heads of steel up to twelve inches in length. They were also armed with swords, Brown Bess muskets, bayonets, pitchforks, guns and pistols, while eight small swivel cannon had been liberated from a navy ship in Bangor. Their equipment may have been rudimentary, but they were determined and they forced their way into Montalto house itself, occupying the mansion. Lord Moira was in England at the time, but the demesne's carpenter, Andrew Brice, was abducted on the afternoon of 12 June and forced to make copies of Monro's proclamation that henceforth no rents would be paid, 'as such rent is confiscated to the use of the National Liberty War'.

As darkness fell, the Crown forces began the bombardment of the demesne and Ednavady Hill. During the attack, explosive shells from the howitzers crashed down on the slate roofs of houses in the streets of Ballynahinch and landed in fields. One shell crashed through the roof of Montalto house causing considerable damage. With their limited supply of ammunition, the rebels returned fire out of the main house at the Monaghans. Some of Monro's officers, including his second adjutant, Dr Valentine Swail from Ballynahinch, argued for a night-time assault because the Monaghans were drinking and plundering the town. But Monro refused to countenance it, believing it would result in serious loss of life. Aside from the difficulty of co-ordinating his troops for a night attack, Monro also appreciated that his soldiers did not have enough ammunition for a sustained assault, so he ordered his men to prepare for an attack on Ballynahinch at first light. His decision turned waverers, who believed that a night-time attack was their only chance of success, into deserters. Several hundred terrified rebels, fearing for their lives, threw down their arms and ran away.

Around 3 a.m., as a pale summer dawn broke across the town and countryside, Monro's artillery sprang into action, opening fire, with Nugent's army replying immediately. The insurgents launched an attack on the Monaghans, and after their ammunition ran out, the weary massed companies pressed forward with their pikes. Soon Nugent's forces gained the upper hand, overwhelming the rebels on Ednavady by early the next morning. As rebels fled the battlefield, pursued by the Monaghans, many were killed. Men were shot by the Dragoons in Montalto's woods, while others were cut down in open country.

Ballynahinch was heavily bombarded and occupied by the Monaghans. Discipline broke down, with scores of soldiers drunk and out of control forcing entry into numerous inns. It was estimated that the cost of the damage by burning, wrecking property and pillaging more than sixty-three houses for up to twelve hours was nearly £20,000. Churches and a total of sixty-nine houses were left standing.

Heavy losses on the rebel side were reported in the town and Nugent decided to withdraw his remaining forces, concentrating them at Windmill Hill. He ordered his bugler to sound a general retreat. But the insurgents mistook the bugle-call, thinking it heralded the arrival of reinforcements and was the signal for the *pas de charge*. At this stage, having already suffered serious casualties from close-range musketry and cannon fire, and with little if any ammunition, the exhausted pikemen faltered before hastily retreating into the countryside.

It is believed that during the fighting up to forty soldiers were killed, although Nugent claimed only six were killed and seventeen wounded. Estimates of those killed on the United Irish side vary, with Nugent reporting that his troops had killed 500 rebels, while many historians suggest that around 300 insurgents died in the battle, with another 200 killed in the relentless pursuit that followed. Whatever the exact numbers, the defeat of the insurgent army at Ballynahinch effectively brought an end to the rebellion in Ulster.

After the battle, the Monaghan militia looted Montalto house before setting part of it on fire, but it was saved by the intervention of Nugent, who was horrified at the burning of a mansion owned by the aristocracy. He instructed Crown forces to bring water from the lake to put out the fire, resulting in an estimated £300-worth of damage – less than might have been the case.

Henry Monro had fled south from Montalto in the direction of Derry townland near Dromara. He was hidden by a farmer for a few days until an amnesty might be declared. But Monro was betrayed to the authorities, court-martialled in Lisburn and sentenced to death.

For her part, Lady Moira, the 2nd earl's mother, who had been living in Dublin, was committed to the rebels' cause and had become a political hostess. She ran the intellectual Moira House Salon, providing a structured forum where women had a leading role, deciding the topics for discussion. It also became an established avant-garde location for poets, musicians and writers engaged in antiquarian studies. During the build-up to the rebellion, the countess entertained senior figures and organisers of the United Irish, including Wolfe Tone, Thomas

Russell, the charismatic leader Lord Edward Fitzgerald, lawyers William Sampson and Thomas Emmet, and his elder brother Robert Emmet. Lady Moira was suspected by the government of assisting the rebels and their sympathisers, but she escaped summary justice.

The Battle of Ballynahinch, and the role that Montalto played, was immortalised in an action painting by Thomas Romney Robinson. Its official title is *Combat between the king's troops and the peasantry at Ballinahinch*, but it is popularly known under its more convenient shorthand name 'The Battle of Ballynahinch'. The atmospheric work, painted from Windmill Hill, depicts soldiers, a few on horseback, some with a howitzer gun, others with heads dipped in mourning as a dead comrade, Captain Henry Evatt, adjutant of the Monaghan militia, who was killed in Ballynahinch, is carried away. Their scarlet and navy military uniforms dominate the foreground, while in the mid-distance sits the white Montalto house surrounded by plantations of trees. The spire of Magheradroll parish church is also visible. The Argyll Fencibles, in their red jackets and trews (a traditional form of tartan trousers), are depicted forming platoon lines and storming through the mill fields to Ednavady where the rebels hold aloft a green flag. On the left of the foreground, members of the yeomanry have captured Hugh McCulloch, soon to be hanged from the sails of the windmill. On the right, General Nugent greets soldiers of the mounted 22nd Dragoons, who have captured a rebel standard. The painting now hangs in the Council of State Room in Áras an Uachtaráin in Dublin's Phoenix Park.

While the fighting in Ballynahinch was the most serious encounter of the northern rising, it was on a different scale to the ferocity that was to occur ten days later south of Dublin. More than 1,500 men, women and children were slaughtered at the Battle of Vinegar Hill in Enniscorthy, County Wexford, on 21 June.

The rebellion was part of the gravest bloodletting in modern Irish history, but by the autumn of 1798 the spirit of insurrection was dead. Lord Moira was so disgusted with his tenants organising a rebellion in his grounds that less than three months after the Battle of Ballynahinch, he put his estate up for sale. He was mercilessly satirised in a ballad that was said to have been written by a fifer in the Drumballroney Volunteers. In reality, it was penned by the Tory statesman George Canning, the future foreign secretary, with the help of the Prime Minister, William Pitt the Younger:

> A certain great statesman whom all of us know,
> In a certain assembly, no long while ago,
> Declared from this maxim he never would flinch,
> 'That no town was so loyal as Ballinahinch.'

> The great statesman, it seems, had perused all their faces
> And been mightily struck with their loyal grimaces;
> While each townsman had sung, like a throstle or finch,
> 'We are all of us loyal at Ballinahinch.'

> The great statesman return'd to his speeches and readings,
> And the Ballinahinchers resum'd their proceedings;
> They had most of them sworn, 'We're all true to the Frinch',
> So loyal a town was this Ballinahinch!

A Flamboyant Legacy (1800–2024)

'The poetry of history lies in the miraculous fact that once, on this earth, once, on this familiar spot of ground, walked other men and women, as actual as we are today, thinking their own thoughts, swayed by their own passions, but now all gone, one generation vanishing after another ...'

George Macaulay Trevelyan,
An Autobiography and Other Essays, 1949

In 1802, four years after the uprising, the Montalto estate was acquired by David Guardi Ker. His ancestors were Scottish Presbyterians and he had relatives living in County Antrim. His family had made their money selling linen in London before moving into the world of finance. Ker invested in land in County Down and bought five townlands around Ballynahinch, as well as the Portavo estate near Groomsport on the Ards peninsula. His family was among the wealthiest in Ireland, and although he bought Montalto for an undisclosed knock-down price, there was uncertainty about what he would do with it. The house had been partially burned in the rebellion, while the town of Ballynahinch was devastated, and Ker's purchase was in effect a fire-sale of damaged property.

Although the Kers were never promoted to the peerage and were not formally an aristocratic family, because of their wealth they became informal members of the nobility, and by 1811 were among the top five landowners in County Down. Since the bulk of their estates was then in south Down, they moved the headquarters of their business from Portavo to Montalto. In 1814 David Guardi Ker married Lady Selina Stewart, the daughter of Lord Londonderry of Mount Stewart, a historic house on the Ards peninsula.

Ker eventually set about making improvements to Montalto house, which included a lengthy process of refurbishment and installing larger windows in accordance with the prevailing fashion. In 1837, during an extremely difficult and often fraught operation, the basement rock under the house and around the foundations was excavated, and a new ground floor created, built in brick and supported by arches and pillars. It seems that this was fashionable at the time, since similar work was carried out at several mansions in Ulster. Excavation work and additions meant that Montalto house appreciably changed its appearance, having been ingeniously converted to a three-storey building. The work was mentioned in the *Ordnance Survey Memoirs* from that year.

The new ground floor consisted of an imposing entrance hall, with eight paired Doric columns, flanked by a library and dining room. A double staircase led up to the *piano nobile*, the main floor, where a long gallery ran the full length of the house, while the sitting room contained renowned eighteenth-century plasterwork. The new floor blended with the existing building and the ground level around the house was lowered to bring the setting into conformity. A new west wing and drawing room were also designed and installed.

By the middle decades of the nineteenth century, the head gardener's position was a senior post on the estate, which also employed a team of plantsmen and labourers. The position of head gardener was held from 1839 by John Stevenson, who helped Ker reorder the landscape, laying out avenues, gardens and plantations, as well as superintending the demesne and carrying out other improvements. It is believed that he was directly involved with the planning and designing of glasshouses built during his period of employment. Stevenson lived in the demesne grounds in Drumnahall House, a solid building with two storeys and a slate roof.

This outdoor appeal of Montalto was torn apart in 1839 when a cataclysmic event destroyed the impressive gardening work and had a devastating effect not only in the estate, but throughout Ireland. Thousands of the demesne's finest trees were uprooted and destroyed during the Night of the Big Wind, *Oíche na Gaoithe Móire*, on 6–7 January. The storm started on a Sunday, the Feast of the Epiphany, but reached the height of its unabated fury in the early hours of Monday morning. In a frightening night, which has lived long in folk memory, hurricane-force winds howled through the grounds, where trees crashed down in the woodlands and surrounding countryside. The grey dawn of a cold winter morning revealed a scene of utter destruction, with thousands of trees lying prostrate and considerable damage caused to rare plants. The exact number of trees damaged has not been quantified, but it was on a considerable scale and, according to contemporary newspaper accounts, may have been up to 10,000. Many of those destroyed were less than seventy years old and were a focus in the demesne. They had been chosen by Lord Moira for the aesthetic beauty of their striking shapes and colours, and for their texture as part of his showpiece demesne. Quite a number were a source of cooling shade in the summer. The path taken by the storm was selective, and various plantations of the more venerable trees, such as mighty oaks and beech survived, but the value of the destroyed timber ran into several thousand pounds.

The suddenness and brutality of the night horrified everyone. To those who recalled the 1798 rebellion it was reminiscent of the thunderous roar of artillery in the estate more than four decades earlier. One description of the wind compared it to being 'like an uninterrupted cannonade'. The scene of destruction also reminded people of the frailty of the natural world in the face of indiscriminate power and the awesome strength of the wind. While living through wild storms in 1796, 1803, 1821 and 1833, no one had witnessed anything on the scale of this one, which far exceeded their experience. 'Those years,' wrote the anonymous author of *A Downpatrick Diary*, were 'little in mischief compared with this'.

Like many towns, Ballynahinch suffered serious damage. A church spire fell through the roof and the Catholic chapel was wrecked. In towns and villages throughout County Down, hovels and small cabins tumbled, while cottages were torn apart, stripped of their thatch, causing widespread distress.

The Night of the Big Wind changed the face of the country. In palatial estates across Ireland, landlords and staff were left to pick up the remains of their ravaged woodlands and try to get back to normality. At Montalto, workers embarked on a programme of clearance, removing fallen or broken trees along with a vast amount of debris. It was many years before the estate was restored to a semblance of normality by a team of gardeners recruited to carry out fresh planting of new bulbs and shrubs. Despite the devastation in the grounds, the mansion had escaped serious damage, but further renovation and improvement work was carried out on it too. A few years later, a Doric portico was built at the front entrance. This was a sheltered area under which a carriage could be driven to protect the occupants from rain.

Six years after the violence of that unforgettable night, Ireland was hit with a much greater act of natural savagery when, from 1845, blight led to the failure of the potato crop year after year, causing the Great Famine. The previous year, David Guardi Ker had died in December at the age of sixty-four. His death led to his son, David Stewart Ker, relocating to Montalto after a serious fire broke out at Portavo, where he had previously been living with his family. Their move came on the eve of the Famine, but there was controversy from the start of Ker's time, as the portico that had been built several years earlier by his father was taken away. The reason for its removal was because neighbouring starving paupers caused what was classified as an 'inconvenience' to the Ker family by taking shelter under it. More than one million people died due to failure of the potato harvest, which lasted from 1845 to 1852, with further depopulation caused through mass emigration.

***

From the late 1840s up to the mid-1850s, significant works were implemented throughout Montalto estate under the guidance of John Stevenson. A collection of outbuildings was demolished and the kitchen gardens relocated, pleasure grounds were created and glasshouses erected where peaches and nectarines were grown. Agricultural investment involved building a mill and stables. Remodelling was also taking place inside the house, leading to an enlarged structure. Part of the work was carried out by the Newtownards builder and architect Charles Campbell. However, tragedy struck in September 1849 when his son, also Charles, was killed in an accident while working in the house. According to contemporary reports, he 'came by his death in consequence of a fall which he received from a scaffold whilst pinning a wall at Montalto House'.

Two decades on from the major rebuilding, David Stewart Ker completed an elegant ballroom, and more than 800 guests were invited to a lavish party for its opening in 1857. This spacious, bright room was where the Kers hung many of their paintings and entertained guests. Montalto had become a celebrated location, not just for its historic battlefield renown but as the scene of high society pleasure and influential dinners. Landowning families dined there, including the Londonderrys, discussing power, politics and money.

During this time of considerable expenditure, the family's fortunes were waning. David Stewart Ker lacked the financial prudence of his predecessors and his ambition outran his income. He harboured an aspiration to be an MP and, at huge financial cost, he was returned as one of the Conservative MPs for Down in the election of 1852. By then, his estate debts exceeded a quarter of a million pounds. His nickname changed from 'Lord Montalto' to

'Six-ties', an epithet derived from his fondness for wearing several scarves or ties at once. Mired in debt, he sold off 4,500 acres in the Landed Estates Court in 1863. But by 1867, by which stage the estate debts had risen alarmingly to £371,000, he had become a heavy drinker, was declared bankrupt and the management of the estates was placed in the hands of trustees.

Around the early 1870s David's son, Alfred Ker, inherited the indebted remains of the Ker estates, but the family had by then slipped into what was regarded as the 'second division' of Irish landowning county gentry. Alfred died in December 1877, aged thirty-four. His brother, Captain Richard William Blackwood Ker (known as Dick), took over control of Montalto. But the estate was being run for the benefit of its creditors, not Ker, with their interests looked after by two trustees. However, Dick still managed to keep up a role in public life and he was High Sheriff of County Down in 1880. The office was an ancient ceremonial and judicial one that then dated back some 800 years, but, regrettably for him, it was unpaid and no public expenses were attached to the duties. A continuing lack of income was now reaching the point of financial crisis and writs were issued for money owing. Dick Ker was also Master of the County Down Staghounds and, in an effort to raise revenue in the 1880s, the kennels in the estate were let to them for £50 per annum, while attempts were made to auction off Montalto's art collection. Ker sold four horses and made efforts to sell 171 pictures advertised as 'Removed from a Mansion in Ireland'.

Despite the financial chaos, by the 1890s the captivating nature of Montalto had become well known, and it was renowned far and wide, attracting artists who wished to depict it. During the final years of the nineteenth century, the house and lake were painted several times in exquisite watercolours by the prestigious Irish artist Joseph William Carey. A member of the Belfast Ramblers' Sketching Club, Carey, whose work was exhibited at the Royal Hibernian Academy in Dublin, was known for his seascapes, as well as paintings of landscapes and mansions. One hundred years after Crown forces had marched from Belfast across the Long Bridge on their way to the Battle of Ballynahinch, Carey captured in an evocative mood the principal route into County Down.

By the end of the nineteenth century, radical developments were taking place in the fortunes of the Ker family. Dick Ker, who was the last of his family to live at Montalto, ended up in the bankruptcy court, with the estate £89,000 in debt. The upkeep of the house was beyond the family, but to sell it would have been regarded as being too humbling. Up until the early twentieth century, occupants of Montalto had supported their lifestyles with rental income from households in Ballynahinch, as well as extensive holdings in surrounding townlands and other parts of County Down. Those who farmed the land were tenants, rather than owners. However, this economic model was undermined by the Wyndham Land Purchase Act (1903), which meant that tenant farmers were able to buy out their leases from their landlords. The transition of the land was agreed between 1905 and 1907, but the 400-acre Montalto home estate was retained. However, successive owners found the agricultural income from this land insufficient to maintain the expenses and the upkeep of the mansion.

In 1910 Dick Ker was forced to put the estate into receivership, and it eventually came under the ownership of Arthur Vesey Meade, 5th Earl of Clanwilliam. He had been aide-de-camp to

Lord Curzon, Viceroy of India, and served in South Africa, where he was severely wounded in the Second Boer War (1899–1902). During the First World War he served with the Royal Horse Guards in France, being mentioned in dispatches and gaining the Military Cross. The 5th earl, who divided his time between Montalto and London, was said to have won the property from Ker in a card game, although this claim has never been substantiated. A family with a stand of Gaelic lineage, the Meades had been long-established in Cork city and the surrounding area. They were descended from Sir John Meade, who represented Dublin University and County Tipperary in the Irish House of Commons, and who was Attorney General to James, Duke of York. Their dynasty was one of fighting men who served the empire either as soldiers or diplomats. The earl's title, a peerage of Ireland, was created in 1776 for John Meade, 1st Viscount Clanwilliam.

The 5th earl needed a new home, as his bride refused to live in Gill Hall, the stately family mansion near Dromore, ten miles west of Ballynahinch, on the grounds that it was overrun with ghosts. Gill Hall was built in the 1670s and from the mid-1700s was owned by the 1st earl, through his marriage to Theodosia Hawkins-Magill. What became known as the 'eerie Beresford ghost story' dated back to October 1693 and the reputed nocturnal appearance of the ghost of John Le Poer, 2nd Earl of Tyrone, to his cousin Nicola Hamilton, Lady Beresford. John appeared to Nicola as an apparition, prophesying that she would die on her forty-seventh birthday. To convince her of the reality of his presence, he grasped her wrist, causing her a permanent scar that she hid beneath a black ribbon. On her forty-seventh birthday, Nicola told her children about the apparition and the prophecy of her death. The children were taken from her and she asked to be left alone in her room. After an hour, the attendants heard screaming and shrieking coming from the room. When they entered, they discovered her body, which bore the same scar tissue all over that marked her wrist, as if she had been burnt alive, and her eyes were bulging from their sockets. The story earned the house the dubious notoriety of being one of the most haunted in Ireland.

Purchasing Montalto for a bargain price of £20,000, Arthur Meade solved one pressing problem by moving home. However, the family's new surroundings were in urgent need of care and attention since the house, and especially the grounds, had fallen into a severely neglected state. Because of a lack of maintenance while under later Ker ownership, some woods had been abandoned, while others were in an extremely poor condition, with rotting trees, decaying plants and abandoned or forgotten gardens. Despite this, during the negotiations for the purchase of the estate, Lord Clanwilliam had refused to sign the agreement unless the plants in the greenhouse – which he saw as being of vital significance in forming part of his horticultural vision for the future – were included in the deal. The sale was supervised by a Downpatrick solicitor, Colonel Robert Hugh Wallace, the agent for the Ker family's creditors.

While the legal niceties and entities were being argued over, on the Irish political stage it was a time of growing tension between nationalists and unionists. With the third Home Rule Bill being published in April 1912, which proposed legislative independence for Ireland, political divisions were sharpening, resulting in the formation of a citizens' militia, the Ulster Volunteer Force, to support the unionist cause. There was no doubting the political outlook of the new occupant of Montalto. In 1913, a year after moving there, Lord Clanwilliam, the Commanding Officer of the 3rd Battalion, Down Regiment, raised the East Down Ulster Volunteers, who used the demesne for training as part of the Home Rule protests. They were addressed by the prominent Irish unionist politician and barrister Sir Edward Carson, who had helped establish the Volunteers. He held political rallies in many towns and attended a 'monster rally' in the grounds of Montalto on 29 July 1913.

At the beginning of February 1914, the East Down Volunteers marched, along with bands and women of the St John Ambulance, from the centre of town to Montalto, where a guard of honour was formed with the leading unionist politician, Captain James Craig, and other guests. This was followed by a reception in the house for the whole company and represented a show of strength and a determination to resist Home Rule by military means. On 6 June the newly formed Ballynahinch volunteers erected a banner at the front entrance gates of Montalto on Dromore Street to celebrate the birth of Lord Clanwilliam's son, who became Lord Gilford. It was the last social occasion before the outbreak of the First World War on 28 July 1914, after which the Volunteers were remoulded into the 36th Ulster Division. It was a tough time for the earl's wife, Lady Muriel, who had to bring up her family alone while her husband was away at war. At the same time, she helped care for wounded Allied officers who convalesced at Montalto.

After the First World War, and in the subsequent partitioning of Ireland, scores of country houses belonging to the Anglo-Irish upper classes were burned down, blown up or destroyed by the IRA. Montalto escaped damage through this turbulent period, and remarkable changes to the grounds lay ahead during the late 1920s and 1930s. Lady Muriel introduced to the estate a large dairy herd of Kerry cattle, believed to be one of the oldest breeds in Europe. During this time, Montalto still had a deer herd, with the County Down Staghounds taking part in hunting them. The family also ran a piggery on the estate and, in their arable farming, the Clanwilliams focused on cereals. The earl was largely an absentee landlord, spending a considerable amount of time in England. However, his wife embraced the upkeep of the grounds through energetic attempts to carry out improvements to the gardens, increasing their size, enhancing their appearance and growing vegetables. A plain rectangular glasshouse, most likely a tomato house or alpine house, was built in concrete with roughcast external walls and its boiler located nearby. In another outhouse, pineapples and melons were grown. In order to protect seedlings and young plants from the harsh weather, cold frames were used to help with growing conditions.

Lady Clanwilliam was prominent in local horticultural circles and enjoyed tending a rock garden brimming with flowers. Such gardens were popular with the wealthy, having come into vogue due to a fashion for travel in the Alps, Dolomites and Pyrenees, and the garden in Montalto was opened to the public for annual charitable fetes, which ran for a decade from 1929. Typically in a rock garden, alpine plants, hardy perennials, dwarf shrubs and bulbs filled the small crevices between randomly placed rocks and stones. Through a decorative rose arbour – formed of a framework for growing roses – Lady Clanwilliam invited friends and neighbours into the grounds, where they admired the colours and fragrant aromas, as well as the grapes in the vinery. As they crossed the rustic wooden footbridge over a small stream, they discussed tropical plants and ferns. On 20 May 1938 the first meeting of the Ulster branch of the Alpine Gardening Society was held at Montalto when an exhibition of alpine plants was staged at a garden fete. Names of those interested in becoming members of the society were noted.

During the Second World War Montalto was utilised in a number of different ways. After the Dunkirk evacuation from the north of France between 26 May and 4 June 1940, a division of a Welsh regiment was moved to the estate to recuperate. Lady Clanwilliam cleared barns and put down bedding for the exhausted soldiers. American service personnel from the 1st Armored Division, nicknamed the 'Old Ironsides', were billeted in the grounds in May 1942, using them for combat training. Montalto was also pressed into service as a vehicle maintenance depot, where women who had joined the armed forces took on the roles of engineers and mechanics, challenging gender norms. During their occupation, and to facilitate the repair of vehicles, soldiers laid a network of concrete roads, resulting in tanks, jeeps and lorries trundling through the grounds and around the streets of Ballynahinch. Elsewhere in the demesne, the soldiers practised digging out trenches on Mutton Hill. While in Montalto they stayed in specially built Navy, Army and Air Force Institute huts, although their commander was provided with superior accommodation in the main house. The vehicles were parked at the Spa back lane entrance, while toilet blocks, storage areas and other buildings were organised. It is said that the original three-acre lake in front of the house, which had deteriorated into a marshy area, was dug out by prisoners of war held in County Down.

A grey mood of despair hung over people in the North. Belfast had been a target for Luftwaffe bombers in the spring of 1941, with three raids in April and May resulting in extensive loss of life. It was a difficult and anxious time for families. After the war, rations on clothes as well as meat, bacon, butter, cheese, tea, sugar and other food continued, while there were shortages of coal and steel. This austerity was echoed in Montalto, where, in the post-war years, the kitchen garden and glasshouses were abandoned, while the paths and grounds fell into disuse or decay, becoming overgrown. Peripheral land was sold off, while other ground was leased to the newly formed Spa Golf Club, leading to the construction of a course.

A description of the house in the 1950s, reprinted in architectural books, provides an insight into the size and number of rooms, shining a light on the immensity of the interior. It consisted of six receptions rooms, a billiard room, eight principal and twelve other bedrooms, five bathrooms, extensive culinary apartments, and was described as being eminently suitable for a hotel, school or hospital. None of these suggested changes of use was embraced, and in 1953 the 6th Earl of Clanwilliam, John Charles Edmund Carson Meade, took up residence, inheriting the estate after the death of his father on 23 January 1953, aged eighty. The 6th earl had fought in the Middle and the Western Desert during the Second World War, later completing his military career as commanding officer of the Tower of London garrison.

Throughout the 1960s people were employed by the estate to help with farming activities, such as grazing, seeding, crop-picking, barley and wheat harvesting and working in the dairy. A foreman, farmhand manager and, twice daily, a team of dairymen milked

150 Friesian cows, all the animals having names. There was a bull house and three silo pits. The 6th earl adopted the role of gentleman farmer, seldom leaving the grounds. Social events were hosted, and each St Patrick's Day the Clanwilliam family entertained the Bishop of Down and local clergy at banquets, while parties were held at Christmas. However, the world of post-war optimism was not felt in Montalto – the earl believed the property was too large and he could not afford the upkeep. Lord Clanwilliam's solution was to demolish sections of the house to try to reduce the rates bill. He knocked down the ballroom and servants' wing, reducing by half the overall size of the building, but he was still unable to make money. His six daughters moved away, and since there was no male line of succession, he put Montalto on the market in March 1979 and retired to Wiltshire.

In April that year a business consortium of John Hogg (timber merchants) and James P. Corry & Son (flax merchants) combined to buy the estate for around £1 million, with plans to run it on a commercial basis. One of their first enterprises was to expand the existing dairy farm with a new complex, housing 300 milking cows, one of the largest and most modern of its type in Ireland. However, in 1986, with the introduction by the European Economic Community of the milk quota system, the company decided to abandon farming and sell off the livestock.

Early in 1985 a dramatic start to the year saw a devastating fire break out in the boiler house in January, which threatened to destroy the mansion. Had it not been for the expertise of firefighters from throughout County Down, it would have been razed. During the operation, fire crews pumped almost the entire contents of the lake into the house, which escaped with substantial smoke and water damage. The worst of the destruction was confined to part of the east wing and rear apartments – the least architecturally valuable sections. After negotiation with the Historic Monuments Council, it was agreed to demolish the damaged part of the east wing and apartments, while the rest of the house was reconstructed.

In 1988 the John Hogg Group became sole owners of the forestry operations when James Corry withdrew from the partnership. Commercial events ranged from holding driven shoots and selling logs to corporate activities and renting Lakeside Cottage, built in the latter half of the twentieth century, to tenants for short-term lets.

The estate was sold to Gordon and June Wilson in 1994, and two years later they moved into the main house. They spent twelve years meticulously restoring the house to its original condition, becoming the fifth dynasty to live there. By any standards it was a daunting task, but the possibilities were exciting. One of the first problems for the new owners was the damage caused by the fire. The east wing was rebuilt with grants from the Historic Monuments Council, and the fabric of rooms was stripped back using original restoration techniques. This included reinstating the 1760s' front-of-house interior cove ceiling, which was in extremely poor condition because the roof was leaking and the plaster was covered in mould. The Wilson family invested money, energy, skill and enthusiasm to preserve the house and the architectural history associated with it, surmounting many complications in their restoration.

Historic houses generally hold traces of their former occupants, and it is clear to see how they have haunted the imagination of the Irish landscape. Stylistically and culturally a walk through Montalto house in the mid-2020s is to wander through a river of time, where the evidence of previous dynasties comes alive in decorative and conservation work. But in Montalto there are no oil portraits on the walls of previous family ancestors. A stroll through the well-appointed library, drawing room and bedrooms shows that the character of the house has been maintained, with doorcases, cornices, mouldings and ceiling roses reflecting craftsmanship and design that speak across the centuries. A highlight is still the lady's sitting room and Robert West's celebrated plasterwork ceiling with squirrels, birds, leaves, vines, peacock feathers and other classical motifs intact.

By 2009 Montalto house had ceased to be the Wilson residence, but the family continued to own and live in the demesne. Plans were in place for an even more ambitious project and a developing process to revitalise the dying grounds. Then, in the midst of the changes around the grounds, the most severe storm to affect Ireland in fifty years, Ophelia, hit the woodlands in autumn 2017, with hurricane-force gusts flattening trees and bringing down a beech planted in 1801. The following year marked a new era. The repurposed demesne was revealed to the public in autumn 2018 as an amenity forest, made up of new gardens, a pinetum and boathouse. More than 30,000 trees were planted along with new flowering shrubs and bulbs, and many different grass species. A fresh energy brought a new dynamism to the running of the demesne.

By the mid-2020s, the gardens planted by Lord Moira had long since melted away, with little or no trace of a horticultural bloodline. But now the floricultural history is once again as compelling as its past, and worthy of the eighteenth-century heritage from which it emanates. In the old Montalto, generations of gardeners, plantsmen and labourers worked hard to realise the potential of the grounds. As part of the succession process, the new Montalto is a triumph of botanical, arboreal and floral multi-tasking, and can be viewed as a haven in which to luxuriate. Set in a romantic and historic landscape, the work of busy hands and clever gardening minds, the multi-layered oasis of floristic diversity is an act of love and obsession. Its design includes an understanding of the roles of balance, contrast, harmony, pattern, symmetry, rhythm and repetition – all the elements that Lord Moira would have approved of more than 240 years ago. Despite the damage wrought by recent storms, there seems little doubt it will continue to thrive into the future.

Part II

The Seasons

Preamble

by Felicity Clements

In the late summer of 1992, our first marital home had sold more quickly than we expected, so Paul and I were looking around for another house to buy. As nothing suitable was on the market we decided to rent whilst continuing the search. I imagined us living for a while in a slick city centre apartment close to work, theatres, restaurants, bars and shopping, with no need to drive anywhere or even have a car. Everything would be on our doorstep – but Paul had other ideas. A country boy at heart, he tentatively suggested renting a cottage on the Montalto estate. Being a city girl through and through, my first thought was that he meant a plush new housing development in Belfast, as I had never heard of the Montalto estate. 'You want us to live in a forest? With no neighbours? On our own?' I was dumbfounded. All I had ever known was life in Belfast, close to my family and friends.

When I realised that Paul was genuinely taken with the idea of renting in the country, I started to think seriously about his suggestion that it could be a great adventure for us. But I kept worrying about the daily drive during the coming winter, when I would be leaving for work in the dark and arriving home in the dark. Paul worked shifts and anti-social hours in his job, so there would be many evenings and overnights when I would be on my own in an isolated cottage, which did not inspire any confidence in me either. To say that I was apprehensive is an understatement. However, when he eventually persuaded me to at least try the cottage, I was so glad he did. I became infected by his enthusiasm for Montalto and the natural world that surrounded us.

For our first few weeks living in the cottage, Paul was off work, recuperating from surgery, so he was always there when I got home from work. He had the fire blazing, dinner on the table and wine opened, making the cottage extremely cosy and welcoming. He told me about his walks around the estate during the day, and the birds and the trees he had seen. At weekends we would explore together, getting lost in the woods. When Paul eventually went back to work, I was so used to living in Montalto that arriving home in the dark to the empty cottage on my own no longer daunted me. Once I was inside with the door locked, curtains closed and the fire lit, I could have been anywhere. In many ways I was safer in the middle of the forest than in any metropolis. I settled into our new existence, relishing the escape from the noises of the city, and started to cherish the sounds of nature.

However, early one morning I was jolted awake. I could not understand why I had woken up so suddenly and then I heard the sound again – a sharp, loud gunshot! I was on my own in the cottage, terrified and too frightened to move or breathe. After a few moments, the rational side of my brain took over and I realised it was the gamekeeper shooting rabbits or foxes in the estate. It took me some time to calm down, get out of bed and make myself several strong cups of tea. We had another early morning awakening a few weeks later that was a much more pleasant experience: a cacophony of birdsong – the dawn chorus – and we rushed outside to listen to it in all its glory. The sound was magical and I have never heard anything like it since.

After my initial hesitation about moving to Montalto, I developed a deep appreciation for our little corner of Utopia. I was far more aware of the changing seasons than I ever had been in the city, and particularly loved the springtime. Watching the awakening of the young buds in the shrubbery and leaves blossoming on the trees was truly a privilege. When we finally bought our new house and were ready to leave the cottage it was a bittersweet time. We were happy to be homeowners again but sorry to leave such a special place.

Autumn

'All the months are crude experiments, out of which the perfect September is made.'

Virginia Woolf, *A Passionate Apprentice:*
The Early Journals, 1897–1909

'I love to see the cottage smoke
Curl upwards through the naked trees,
The pigeons nestled round the cote
On dull November days like these.'

John Clare, 'Autumn'

From the moment I set eyes on Montalto, I know I will get on well with it. We arrive when it is verging on autumn, with the last vestiges of summer hanging in the air. For a year, a small, damp cottage in the woods during one of the coldest and most severe winters in living memory is to become home for myself and my wife, Felicity. Having been saturated in an urban culture, living in three different cities over fifteen years, we had lost sight of nature, of the fiery colours of autumn and of night skies filled with stars. More shack than chic, our cottage is basic, with several bedrooms, an antiquated kitchen and 'cosy' living room, which, at a squeeze, just about holds a settee and table. But for all the lack of comfort and modernity, Lakeside Cottage, an L-shaped building in the middle of the demesne, is an idyllic location.

Set in the heart of the County Down countryside, the Montalto estate is on the edge of Ballynahinch, a fifteen-minute walk from town, or two minutes as the common starling – *Sturnus vulgaris* – flies. The demesne represents a get-away-from-it-all escape, a place to apprise arboreal life with its enchanting groves of trees. It is closed to the public when we take up residence in 1992, only two years before it is purchased by the Wilson family. The result is that more animals than people are in evidence. With its community of wildlife, it is a world in miniature, a universe of its own, and a tranquil preserve in which to watch unfolding episodes of nature, sometimes on a grand scale, other times on a microscale. During our stay, the winds would reach cyclonic proportions, with the ever-present prospect of ancient trees falling on the cottage. Initially we plan to spend six months here while waiting to buy another house, but the search takes longer than anticipated and our stay stretches to a year, rewarding us with vignettes of natural wonder.

Aside from birds, insects and mammals, we share the surroundings with just two other people living in the grounds: a gamekeeper and a groundsman. 'You'll have the place to yourselves and will see things that will live with you for the rest of your life,' the gamekeeper tells me prophetically on the first day, adding a caveat, 'Just look out for the fox traps on your rambles and large brown rats scampering across paths.' Strictly speaking, we do not have it to ourselves, since we are surrounded by a veritable menagerie of creatures. However, we are free of dog-walkers and joggers, as well as the roar of motorbikes, trucks and buses, police and fire sirens, and the noise pollution of a multitude of burglar and car alarms. We do not realise how lucky we are, and from the outset I record in my journal notes of what I see and hear, so that I will remember the experience. I want to acknowledge our surroundings, giving them the respect they deserve.

The cottage is a small, pebble-dashed building round the corner from a lake. The adjacent lawn leads to the big house, its somewhat gaunt appearance dominating the demesne. Built after the Second World War, the cottage was later occupied by the family of dairymen connected to the estate, and at various times was rented out by the owners. We are the latest fortunate residents to rent the cottage, to revel in the silence, live adjacent to the earthy scenes of ancient trees and watch the breakfast feeding habits of birds and squirrels through our window each morning. The lake itself, from which the cottage takes its name, projects a serene appearance and has just been dredged and stocked with trout. A local fishing company is using it to develop and assess their products, although most of the time it does not appear to be in use.

The first thing I hear on a bright morning in mid-September, a week before the autumn equinox, is a rasping bark from what sounds like a dog up a tree but turns out to be one of the most affecting of all creatures, a cocky grey squirrel. Constantly busy, the animals – both grey and red varieties – perform rounds of gymnastics in the pine trees that stand tall across the drive from our new home. They are running errands, scrambling for food to stash, and scuttling about their business in a purposeful manner, chattering as they go. There is always a task in hand and a job to be done. The squirrels are now creating their winter dreys, but the search for food, which involves sniffing out conkers, snaffling chestnuts and wolfing down hazelnuts, is a priority. Their shopping list contains seeds, berries, buds, flower-shoots and even the sap of a tree under the bark. Luckily for them, they do not have to go into town for provisions since their food supply is easy to come by.

The inquisitive squirrels greet the first day of our new woodland lifestyle. Over an alfresco morning coffee, I observe a posse of them clambering up trunks in jerky movements, slithering from branch to branch, spinning through 180 degrees. Binoculars bring their distinguishing features into sharp definition: ginger face, enlarged erect ears, wide beady eyes and whiskers twitching as they adopt an otherwise motionless position, checking on their surroundings. Energetically, they flick their bushy tails, moving up trunks and running nimbly along thick branches with acrobatic aplomb. Then they stop, look around and stare into the distance, giving another defiant bark, a sign that they are becoming excited or feel under threat. I wonder if they can see me watching them from the garden bench, or if they even care, although I am convinced that one is fixing me with an imperious glare that soon morphs into supreme indifference. There is a moment of hilarity when one squirrel leaps for a branch but misjudges the distance, failing to make it, resulting in a *husk-husk-qaaaa* alarm call. Grey squirrels, *Sciurus carolinensis*, from the Greek *skia* (shadow) and *oura* (tail), are more dominant, and over the next year I will come to be on nodding terms with them, but for now, with a hop, skip and jump, they are gone.

Shortly before our house move, I had taken a month's leave from work to recover from a hernia operation. It was not a major surgical procedure, and I was in hospital for just a number of days. However, on the advice of my doctor, I had taken time off to recover and he suggested it was best not to drive for four weeks. What better place in which to be a prisoner, I silently wonder, than a cottage in a wooded demesne? It gives me the luxury of having time to absorb my surroundings and acclimatise to the woods, enjoying the onrush of autumn. The result is that I follow the laissez-faire approach of wandering aimlessly around, as recommended by the gamekeeper. Soon I recover to full walking health, rediscovering the dictum *solvitur ambulando*: 'It is solved by walking.'

Prior to living on the estate, I had a fragmentary knowledge of birds, familiar mostly with the common garden or parkland variety, but I am aware that by instinct birds are drawn to woodlands. Within the first few days, as I perch unobtrusively on a log in the early afternoon wondering about the future of two old trees that are bent over to forty-five degrees from the weight of time, I interpret the short, repeated *tswee-wooo* tinkly autumnal song of robins as a friendly welcome. The wind ripples through the topmost leaves of the trees. A goldcrest, Ireland's smallest bird, flickers in the foliage, clocks me and leaves quickly. Newly arrived birds are playing a game of hide-and-seek, but the mechanical, flinting *tchack-tchack* of what I call a 't-jackdaw' is followed by its bursting out of the canopy.

My next encounter from the thickets of tree-cover stops me in my tracks. Ducking behind a large pine tree, I sense an inhospitable undertone to my eavesdropping and instinctively know that I am being scrutinised. An unidentifiable bird chirps out its harsh machine-gun rattle, a disdainful call sounding remarkably equivalent to the words *clear off! clear off!*, while a pigeon heckles me with a condescending and thrice monotonous *yoo-hoo-yoo-hoo-yoo-hoo*. Well-wooded places are to be cherished, but the indignant bird noises are designed to let me know that they are aware of my presence. As a blow-in, I ponder my invasion of the birds' theatrical platform, an interloper come to stare, to live among them, listen to their chittering and breathe their forest air. While they may not like the cut of my jib and regard me as an intruder, in my defence I am a short-term leaseholder in their kingdom, aware at the outset that this is *their* playground and hunting enclave. I have come in peace with my binoculars and bring no harm, which may not be the way they see it. The clap from the wings of a feral pigeon rising in exuberant flight to the crown of a tree provides a reassuring acceptance.

Birdsong has a lilting quality but there is also a melancholy feel to some of the singing, hesitant with short phrasing and pausing. My presence may have spooked the birds, but I get the distinct impression that they are fond of lurking behind leaf-covered branches. Some birds forage on the ground, then sing from the tops of trees, their proclamation of territory warding off the stranger in their midst. As I mull over my intense trespass, another loud repetitive sound sidetracks me: *teeech-chuh-teeech-chuh-teeech-chuh* – a great tit testing its vocal cords. I cannot see it because of the impenetrable thickness of tree cover, but I am familiar with the sound, which comes across like the din of a rusty wheelbarrow, or a bicycle pump being used.

Summer birds, such as swifts, swallows and house martins, have departed for warmer climes because their food supply of insects and butterflies has dried up. But there is a quiet energy as the topographical residents including robins, tits, finches and wrens all fidget around while crows and rooks swerve their high-speed way through trees.

On my part, there is an element of what is known in Irish as *aduantas*, a feeling of unease or discombobulation, at being in unfamiliar surroundings. Although I do not perceive myself as an outsider, my new environment is a startling contrast from the constant assault of traffic and bustle of a city. There is considerable life all around, some of it hidden, or at least hiding in plain sight, while other creatures may be unheard, untouched or un-smelt. There is also interconnectivity between the birds and other animals that live here, and their link to trees and plants. However, for me, this is a leap into the unknown, an attempt to get closer to the wild, to eyeball birds infrequently found in back gardens or parks. I am conscious of a quotation from Gilbert White, the English 'parson-naturalist', ecologist and bird lover: 'The language of birds is very ancient, and, like other ancient modes of speech, very elliptical: little is said, but much is meant and understood.'

I do not have a scientific background and, aside from identifying common birds, have limited knowledge of the different species. Reading the field guides is a long way from the reality of seeing birds, so over several recent winters I had joined extra-curricular evening classes to build up my birdwatching awareness, participating in Sunday field trips, although these were often washed out by heavy rain. All this was frustrating and accomplished little in enhancing my understanding of the creatures of the air. In fact, it led me to the realisation that seeing birds is a game of luck, since it depends on factors such as the weather, being in the right place at the right time, and pure happenstance – not forgetting local knowledge and knowing where and when to go to specific locations. Moreover, birds do not seek you out – you must seek them out, learning to be quick of eye and of ear, allied by the need to remain still. The big problem with birds is that one moment they are here, the next moment they are gone, and a sighting may last a mere millisecond. For these reasons, I have come to regard myself as a novice birdwatcher.

The birds' tunefulness is another matter. Each species has its own suite of unique songs, or even a subsong differing from autumn to spring. It is a private language known to those who listen carefully, free of noise and human conversation. There are alarm calls, contact calls, complex melodies or combinations of sounds to impress mates or maintain pair bonding in courtship; there are whistles of love or territorial cries of warning; there are birds that mimic others, those that laugh loud and those with unique phrases or speech patterns. Decoding the cacophony of these ear-catching songs is the key to their identification and appreciation of their behaviour, habits and actions, but presents challenges. Undaunted, I arm myself with practical field guides that help with song recognition, among other things. The sheer variety of birds, their lingua franca and level of detail are overpowering, and by their nature the books deal in generalities. The explanations of tail, leg and eye colour, as well as body and bill shape, posture, plumage and preening – although highly colourful – constitute an esoteric language, off-putting to newcomers:

Brownish mask with a white supercilium.

Blue grey mantle extends up the nape.

White speculum on secondary flight feathers, wing bars, white patch.

Chestnut stripes on scapulars and sides of mantle.

Diagnostic pale wing bars on the median and coverts.

The description is complemented with a host of references to upper-parts, underparts and outer-parts, feather pattern recognition and minutiae such as moulting, distribution, migration timing, subtleties of shading, eyebrow prominence and habitat usage. They include thumbnail poses of the birds, but as I turn the pages, I call to mind a character in Samuel Beckett's *Molloy*: 'Here is something I can study all my life, and never understand.'

While it is hard to capture descriptions of birds in the covers of a book, my curiosity is coupled with a willingness to learn and a determination to improve my fieldcraft by devoting time to building up my latent knowledge of what is known as 'Jizz'. This is an acronym used to help with the identification of birds by describing their overall impression or appearance, linked to size, colour, combining voice, habitat and location. It is a corruption of 'Giss', meaning 'General Impression of Size and Shape', used to identify military aircraft during the Second World War. Another aspect of which I hope to learn more is 'ornithomancy', the practice of reading omens from the flight and cries of birds, once thought to convey messages from the gods.

Natural history books, including bird guides, are detached and scientific, classifying and cataloguing. In nature writing, however, the feelings of observers are often part of what they write about, frequently giving an emotional response to what they see or hear. While writing about nature is still rooted in realism, it may also be impressionistic, lending itself to purple prose and a leap of the imagination. The most important aspect to it is that writers put centre-stage the interconnections between nature and humans. In Evelyn Waugh's exuberantly comic novel *Scoop* (1938), his character William Boot contributed nature notes to Lord Copper's *Daily Beast*. A sentence from one of his countryside columns, 'Feather-footed through the plashy fen passes the questing vole', is a celebrated example of overblown prose written to literary effect.

Numerous poets have had love affairs with the natural world, and while I do not write poetry, their elegiac work inspires me, their words frequently ringing in my ears. Robert Frost once wrote that, 'He would like to lodge a few poems in the minds of people where they can't be got rid of', something with which I empathise. Many writers of nature explore the joining of ecology and the imagination, and since 2000 there has been an explosion of interest in the subject in Ireland and Britain. This often involves the discovery of exoticism in the familiar and, through detailed observation of the landscape, seeing the extraordinary in the ordinary, such as in the work of writers including Henry David Thoreau, Michael Viney, Nan Shepherd, Tim Robinson, Ed Abbey, Barry Lopez and Robert Macfarlane.

The forest flora of Montalto intrigues me. In the early 1990s my interest in wildflowers blossomed when I developed amateurish botanical leanings, particularly because I was touring Ireland for my travel books and becoming acquainted with the Burren of County Clare. The flowers there are Arctic, alpine and Mediterranean, growing in limestone beside the coast. Marvelling at their names brought a realisation of the importance of correct identification and the fact that naming adds lustre to writing: *Gentiana verna*, *Dryas octopetala* and *Geranium sanguineum* are just three of the Latin binomials with which I became familiar and which have stayed with me. I especially like their *gestalt* and the way they roll mellifluously off the tongue. This, in turn, led me to try to understand how woodland flowers get their names, bringing a fresh perspective. To know their stories and legends is a peek into the past and connects us with our forebears but also with the plants in a much more meaningful way.

At either side of the mansion, rampant rhododendrons blaze their way into the picture alongside laurels and a mini-jungle of greenery. Dense bushes of white, purple and crimson rhododendron are flowering, with thick vegetation taking over one side in particular, although some look past their best. Often in large estates *Rhododendron ponticum* was planted for ornamental purposes in the late eighteenth century to brighten up woodlands. Some regard it as native, but, in fact, it was introduced from Asia and parts of Europe. It spreads fast, is hard to keep under control and has an invasive potential, strangling native woodland. Gardeners consider it a pest or pernicious weed because its leaves are toxic to other plants and it can repel wildlife. In Montalto the rhododendron is all-pervasive, bringing colour and providing cover for game birds.

To the left of the house, one of the estate's oldest trees, a giant redwood sequoia with spongy bark, thrives in an embankment. The main avenue, off Dromore Street leading into the grounds, is dressed in a handsome run of mature lime trees, as well as chestnut and sycamore, interspersed with laurel and ferns, all planted to impress visitors in their carriages in earlier centuries. The big house is dominated by a large lawn the size of a football pitch, and the lake is bordered by fading blooms of water lilies and gunnera. Trees surround the back and sides of the house, while a champion sycamore growing on the lawn is noted as a magnificent specimen for its size and age. Other champion trees in the grounds, such as liquidambar, are thought to date from the late 1700s, and may have been the seedlings that came from the West Indies during Lord Moira's time.

Catch the right day of reflective autumnal sunshine and, from a far-off vantage point, a widescreen image of the elegantly proportioned house is reproduced in the water of the lake, which has barely a ripple across its silver surface. With the surrounding trees and shrubbery, it is a perfect likeness, a calming cinematic viewing experience. It brings to mind a reflective moment captured in Henry David Thoreau's *Walden*: 'A lake is the landscape's most beautiful and expressive feature. It is earth's eye; looking into which the beholder measures the depth of his own nature.'

With time on my hands, I explore parts of the 400 acres around me. Wandering along the numerous narrow paths and tracks without planning a route, leads to a giddy aimlessness with no fixed destination and an appreciation of the mix of verdant September colours. We have been here for one week, and already there is an out-of-this-world enchantment. Most flowers are either shrivelled or hunkering down, while wrens search for food. The woodland floor teems with fungi, including the sticky red exuberance of beefsteak fungus and ghostly-looking porcelain mushrooms. Another sign of autumn is the fall of birch seed, which is dispersed by the wind. Each individual tree is able to create thousands of tiny seeds, and the air is full of them.

By the end of our second week, we have settled into our new home in the depths of the forest. The three days, 20, 21 and 22 September, have a reputation that is reflected in an old folklore saying, 'September blow soft, till the fruit's in the loft', leading to the hope that the fruit harvest could be gathered during calm weather. Berries on the rowan and the hawthorn are turning red, while acorns on oak trees slowly darken from pale creamy green to golden brown. On the autumn equinox the sun rises calmly due east of us and sets due west. It is an alluring intermezzo, but from now on daylight hours start to grow shorter as we ease ourselves into October, with the winter solstice ahead on 21 December.

The familiar perfumes of wet twigs, damp ground leaf mulch and blackberries are becoming part of our stay as we prepare for darker nights. Another of the estate's champion trees, and one of the most famous in the grounds, is a liquidambar Austrian pine, boasting the biggest Irish girth of its species. In the pinetum, a giant redwood is said to be the tallest, oldest and largest example of the species in Ireland, and has the largest girth of its type recorded in the North, lending it historical and horticultural importance.

Around the grounds, pheasants skulk amid the dark foliage, as well as a covey of partridges. Both birds emerge occasionally from the undergrowth flying through the woods or fields. *Alectoris rufa* (red-leg partridge) are cousins of the grey or English partridge, and the male incubates and rears the second clutch the female sometimes lays. The partridges are brought up on the estate in captivity and held in pens to keep vermin, such as stoats, away from them. During autumn and early winter, up until the end of January, the birds are reared and then, at six weeks old, released into the fields for driven shoots. They are rotund animals, wandering around crouching and hiding, sometimes in the small rock garden beside our cottage. Echoing around the grounds, they out-crow each other with their loud *ka-chu-chu*. Their wings flap to comic effect when they call, unconcerned about drawing attention to themselves. With their white chin, black necklace and conspicuous pinkish red legs, they are also called French partridges, known to the log-cutters as 'Frenchmen'.

From our living room we have a grandstand view of these playful birds, flying, wandering or hopping past. The 'red legs' are widespread, on the paths or lurking behind trees. They perch in the trees too, sometimes making a half-hearted effort to fly on to the roofs of adjoining outbuildings, but they prefer the ground to heights. In the morning, they indulge in to-ing, fro-ing and darting energetically across the lawn, appearing magically from shrubs and plants. On occasion, they gather around in a harem, peering out suspiciously from the undergrowth. Understandably, they look worried when they see us, in case our form of nature involves an act of random bloodlust.

The knockings of autumn are making themselves heard in the rustle of the leaves and whistle of the chilly wind. At the front of the house the grass is covered in dew, while the gossamer of a cluster of cobwebs on the hedges lends a purity and freshness. In the fleeting morning sunshine, the webs light up in twinkling displays. Moisture caused by condensation of water vapour hangs from silky threads like shimmering pearls, creating a glitter effect.

Although October starts brightly, temperatures soon fall. A sense of melancholy marks the middle of the month, or to be precise 18 October, St Luke's Day, said to bring calm, warm weather. According to legend, St Luke was annoyed at being overshadowed by other saints' days, so to avoid being forgotten he brought a welcome spell of mild days in the middle of autumn, later described by the expression 'Indian summer'. There is no sun on this day, but the estate is enveloped in a bronze sheen with autumn now well into its stride. Thousands of acorns lie across the forest floor, while leaves on beech and birch are in the throes of changing colour. In a note in my journal I list the following shades: deep orange, brown and amber, buttery yellow and lemon, rufous, ochre, vivid gold, blood-red, russet and endless variables.

It may well be St Luke's 'Little Summer', but the songs of the birds have faded, although robins are still producing melodious, wistful notes. Montalto's corvid population of rooks, magpies, jackdaws and hooded crows (known as 'hoodies') is in a healthy state. In areas of Britain hooded crows are called carrion or scald crows, but in parts of the north of Ireland and north-west Scotland, they wear a grey jerkin, which is how they came to adopt the nickname 'hoodie'. Rooks search the ground for earthworms, as well as the larvae of daddy-longlegs. Then they fly up to rest and digest before returning to feed again. Other birds are busy establishing and defending territories by reducing competition in order to ensure access to ample sustenance.

'Leaf-peepers', a term I first came across during a trip to New England, are aware of the visual treat in the turning of the seasons. It is especially strong in late autumn, marking the last bursts of colour before the onset of winter. The front lawn is criss-crossed by flights of insects and a few listless end-of-season wasps, while a colony of flying ants swarms surprisingly in a corner near the lake. Ants may not be everyone's favourite insect, but they are part of nature's 'undertaker' team, cleaning up and recycling the remains of small dead animals and returning nutrients to the environment. The subtle orange of the bark on the trunk of a Scots pine is just one of the pleasures on a woodland walk, while a secret overgrown garden is on our doorstep. Hedgerows are full to the brim with hawthorn berries, suggesting plenty of feasting for the numerous birds and small mammals that rely on them.

On the radio news this morning, I hear that the air traffic controllers are striking, but this has no bearing on the Montalto airspace, where increasing activity is discernible. Leaves swirl to the ground from surrounding trees, making it easier to watch birdlife. True to its name, a treecreeper, spiralling mouse-like up the trunk, probes the bark's wrinkled skin, pausing, sniffing, prising insects and, with tiny purposeful hops, moving at a snail's pace. Treecreepers are inconspicuous, which is why they are known as the 'ghost' birds of the woods. Their thin, high-pitched whistle is barely audible. If there is a contender for 'best camouflaged bird' it would win easily, and I notice this one only because a flake of bark comes alive. With a streaky dark-brown back and stiff, stubby tail, the treecreeper is well-nigh invisible, but its brilliant silvery-white belly provides a flashy glimpse and wonderstruck moment. On the premise that what goes up must come down, I watch as the bird takes off, floating to the bottom of a neighbouring tree to then resume its foraging ascent. With their downcurved needle bill, treecreepers search and listen carefully for insects in the interstices of the bark. They build cosy nests high up in the trees, hidden by branches, and I am unable to get close enough to see them.

Solitary birds such as the treecreeper are tantalisingly glimpsed and understandably wary of humans, so consequently they are content to remain inconspicuous. But this is unequivocally not the case with the delicate long-tailed tits, the social antitheses of the 'creepers. Their high-pitched yet soft *tseep-tseep-tseep* call, made to each other, stops me in my tracks on a path less than half a kilometre from the cottage. Foraging en masse and swarming into several trees, they are a tribal party, and with their ceaseless activity it is hard to count them. This is an amalgam of two or three families, with up to twenty birds plainly visible. Jumping from branch to branch, muttering quietly to one another, dangling like trapeze artists in a circus act, they ransack each twig for morsels. Soon the birds are within touching distance, yet completely unfazed by my presence less than a metre from them. They treat me as though I am a part of the landscape, and the fact that I am standing in front of them is not causing them to change their behaviour. It is an intimate sighting of a gregarious and loose feeding flock, known as a volery, which I take pleasure in identifying; although their extremely long tails are a giveaway, it is still a small triumph. As they like company and there is an element of safety in numbers, the brood remains together for the autumn and winter.

I look several of the small tits in the eye, observing their flicking tail feathers as they dart around with furtive glances. At five and a half inches (14 cm) long, half their length is made up of their tail, measuring more than three inches. Long-tailed tits have a close-knit family life which is vital for their survival. With their thin whispers, clicks and whistles, they are especially vocal and stay connected at this time of year. Often overlooked or unnoticed by walkers, the birds are a mixture of striking patterns, with deep brown plumage, cream and pinkish above with pale pink below, while a dark stripe runs from the base of their bill above the eye.

There are a variety of folk names for these endearing creatures, such as jack-in-a-bottle, hedge mumruffin, bottle tit, oven bird, fuffit, prinpriddle and 'flying teaspoons'. In his poem 'Birds Nesting', John Clare gave them an especially evocative name: 'I have seen bumbarrels on the wing / Full twenty flitting in a lot / And now and then on branches hang / Then peck and seek another spot.'

Eventually they take off, engaging in a 'follow-my-leader' flight path. I delight in close-ups with dozens of other birds in Montalto, but my brief encounter with these small charismatic and frolicsome *Aegithalos caudatus* lives with me. It heightens my awareness that the best way to understand nature is to spend time in its company; it matters little if it is wolf-watching, studying brown bears or glimpsing the flight of a majestic sea eagle. On another walk, I locate the tits' nest, made from a mixture of moss, wool and feathers, bound together with gossamer. Not wanting to intrude on their privacy, I leave them to nest in peace.

There is often an element of surprise in the appearance of a sudden flurry of birds – the 'finch gang', as they become known to us – and I have watched them moving all together through parts of the grounds. The chaffinch song echoes the pink breast colour of the male because to my ears it sounds like a cross between *pink-pink* and *finch-finch*, while the bullfinch has a quieter *deu-deu* woodwind note.

In early evening, as the crepuscular light drains from the sky into semi-darkness, or half-light, and after the workers finish their day's labour cutting logs at the farm buildings, parties of glamorous goldfinches begin their ostentatious show. With their distinctive bright red heads, black cap and yellow wing stripes, they create a splash of colour at the back of the barn beside the cottage. Frequently a charm of the birds – an apt collective noun – materialises from nowhere pre-twilight. Sociable but restless, they shin up trees and fling themselves around, calling to each other in rapid flight, before taking up position on wooden posts. Their musical tinkling reminds me of the sound of metallic coins, their calls both innocent and uplifting. They used to be known as 'thistle finches' and during the nineteenth century were popular as caged birds. Hungrily, they embark on a smash-and-grab raid, winkling out thistle and teasel seeds, pressing open the scales of the larch to gorge on food.

Goldfinches are also called 'redcaps', or occasionally their folk name 'thistle-tweakers' is invoked due to their love of seeds, with the grounds around the sheds offering ready-made nourishment. Because of their flashiness, *Carduelis carduelis*, or in Irish *Lasair choille*, is referred to as the 'flame of the forest'. The gamekeeper puts out edible quinoa seeds which attract the finches. They enliven the surroundings with a freshness, adding a dash of colour as one of the most striking of all Montalto's birds. Frequently, I catch fleeting sight of them drifting through the woods in their erratic flight, keeping up their call notes, more often heard than seen.

During this tantalising time in the transition of late afternoon to nightfall, which we label 'twilight o'clock' or 'goldfinch o'clock', the air is filled with the incense of resin from the sawn trunks. The loose dusk chorus, accompanied by mellow golden light, is a favourite time when a strange, spirit-reviving calm descends. In fading light on my early evening rounds, a barn owl floats slowly into the far distance, a silent ghost on a low-flying quest. Across in the woods, a soft creaking or plaintive whistle emanates from bullfinches. Shy birds, they are hard to catch in sharp focus but enjoy nibbling on the buds of fruit trees. I discover the collective noun for a flock is the congenial term 'a bellowing of bullfinches'. Nearby the twittering song of a greenfinch, which turns into a wheeze, competes with house sparrows in the noise-filled airspace.

There is an evanescent magic to twilight. Before it dissolves into the nebulous approaching darkness of night-time, the gradually declining light is known by the expressive term 'dayligone' or 'dimity'. It marks a special time when the sky is clear until the point when a solitary star switches on. In Irish this is known as *idirsholas* (interlight) or *amhdhorchacht* (darkness), while the French express it as *L'heure bleue*, a dissolving timespan beloved of Impressionist painters, such as Vincent van Gogh and Camille Pissarro. In his poem 'He wishes for the Cloths of Heaven', W.B. Yeats summed up this time: 'The blue and the dim and the dark cloths / Of night and light and the half-light'. The Irish writer Robert Lynd, who was familiar with Yeats' poetry, thought that the twilight of dusk was the best time to admire the landscape anywhere in the country:

> There is one thing which gives a unity – a personality as it were – to Ireland. It is the glory of light which comes towards evening and rests on every field and every hill like a strange tide. Everywhere in Ireland, north, south, east, and west, the evening air is, as a fine living poet has perceived, a shimmer as of diamonds.

For now, the silent birds are roosting. Other creatures have also retreated to their nests and bedded down, and a quietude envelops the estate; the bewitching time has gone to dark with the lights turned out. During cold November days I find myself disagreeing with what the nineteenth-century poet Thomas Hood sardonically wrote about the month: 'No sun, no moon! no morn, no noon, / No dawn, no dusk, no proper time of day, / No shade, no shine, no butterflies, no bees, / No fruits, no flowers, no leaves, no birds! – / November!'

The November sun is certainly low, its power vanquished, at best a fleeting tokenistic glimpse. Despite the melancholy gloom, and while bees and butterflies are hard to find, there is no shortage of birdlife and leaves. I jot down a list of the things I catch glimpses of on my November walks, everyday audio utterances accompanied by brief sightings, assigning them to declarative journal notes:

Lacklustre sparrow-ese chattering from rooftops before performing pirouettes.

A pair of buzzards soaring slowly high above the forest searching for birds.

High-pitched piping *tsuu-tsuu-tsuu* of a gang of coal tits cutting through trees.

Wood pigeons squawking and fossicking with a brouhaha around high hedges.

Vociferous *chink-chink* of a blackbird permeating the woodland.

Birds are now feeding in earnest for the lean months ahead. By the second week of November, with the weather still noticeably dull but mild, temperatures average twelve degrees Celsius. Forecasters describe this calm weather under the term 'St Martin's Summer', commemorating the saint's feast day, 11 November. That day starts with a pleasant morning at the cottage although by late afternoon with darkness falling, the wind is gathering momentum and susurrating through trees.

On a stroll through the woods, the sound of a stick breaking underfoot is like the sharp crack of a pistol. A damp, grey murkiness hangs over the trees, filling the forest with mist, while a deep hush settles in as the creatures prepare for winter. Ivy climbs up the boles of trees, which the insect population appears to love. Once in a while, the high-pitched whine of a chainsaw cuts through the silence as the log-men fill bags of wood for the winter. Straggling flowers, including herb robert, survive, and scarlet berries decorate hedges and bushes. Plump bluebottles are active, but we steer them out of the cottage because they are a loud nuisance and lay larvae. Boasting one of the most rhythmically curious names that I have come across in the scientific world – *Calliphora vomitoria* – they are on a search for nectar.

Like confetti, one at a time, the leaves are in free fall as they pirouette and zigzag their way to the ground in see-sawing descents, resting delicately on an ever-growing mound of vari-coloured carpet. Autumn, coming from the Latin *autumnus*, a personification of maturity and manliness used in the sixteenth century, has long intrigued me. The word 'fall', beloved of Americans, is from old Germanic languages and refers to the fall of the leaf and the fall of the year. Emigrants to the British colonies in North America brought the term fall with them, and it stayed.

As sunlight decreases and the nights get cooler, leaves can no longer produce the food they need. The chemical chlorophyll, which gives the leaves their green tint, is now disappearing and yellow and orange colours hidden under the green are showing. I had noticed on my walks the striking colour differences in specific sections of the trees. Leaves on one side at the top of the canopy appear to turn a cherry red or brown long before those on the lower side.

At November's end, as autumn draws to a close, the trees have shed their ballgowns and we reflect on our first season. It has been a mix of wet, sharply cold, sometimes mild and occasionally dry weather. Now is the best time to embrace the multi-coloured display of fallen leaves, the leaf-lorn state of the trees, the crinkle underfoot and the earthy smell.

On our travels over the years my wife and I haggled for carpets in Kashmir, Marrakesh, the Covered Market in Istanbul and other Middle-East locations. The carpets' vibrant colours have been part of our life together. A shrewd seller in Srinagar told us the oriental carpet that we bought from him had been 'waiting for us'. It would, he assured us, be our best ever purchase and every day it would remind us of our honeymoon. The mounds of crisp leaves on the woodland floor and the lawn resemble a similar array of flamboyant pigments: the depth of their shades ranging from the dark-tan and rust-brown hues of oak leaves, some heavily speckled, in one corner of woodland, to the startlingly brilliant golden yellow and orange of wispy birch trees.

By any stretch of the painterly colour chart, the leaf litter represents a spectacular smorgasbord, with the intense redness of the copper beech standing out, while other dominant shades run through the colour spectrum of deep purple to pink. Smaller trees and shrubs along the edge of the lake produce warm brown and viridescent leaves, a sign that the tree is alive and well. The mosaic of colours is dictated by the length of daylight, the water and the minerals, especially phosphate, which have fuelled the photosynthesis during the summer.

Bare trees, with deeply grooved brown bark, mean that we can see farther than at any time since our arrival. It is beneficial for trees to shed leaves since it preserves the moisture in their branches and trunk and prevents them from drying out and dying. Leafless trees are in a stronger position to tolerate winter storms as fierce winds move through them more easily. I push aside bare branches, and raindrops fall on my anorak. With a swish of my trainers, I scuff through thick heaps of leaves – up to six inches in depth – scattering them in all directions. In the overlapping mixture of leaf piles I glimpse a rapidly disappearing beetle and a leaf miner. The leaves appear to be in conversation with each other and I am in thrall to the variety of their size and shape. It is like walking on rich, feathered mats. I study them in detail, but I am not the only one engrossed in them – at another pile a hungry wood pigeon pecks its way through them in search of food. As it moves slowly, it peers up into the distance when it hears a noise, returning to poke concentratedly around, before lifting off for an elevated, gimlet-eyed view from a branch.

My rustling transports me to childhood, the mile-long walk each morning to get to primary school and an autumn memory that was drummed into us: evergreen trees keep their leaves while deciduous trees drop their leaves. With our satchels, we followed a tree-lined footpath, close to the River Blackwater in Tyrone, which each November was smothered in leaves. It was a show-stopping moment and, to the consternation of the teachers, meant that it took longer than normal to reach the school gates as we constantly whooshed back and forward through the piles – the clarity of the bell piercing our fun as we headed to class. As the writer Benedict Kiely once stated: 'Every country-reared man knows that anything he ever learned, of good or bad, was learned not in a classroom but while idling along the road from school.'

We may not have known, or even cared, as we crept to the school gates in those happy-go-lucky days, that fallen leaves provide important bacteria for beetles and for a community of mites, millipedes and earthworms, which help assimilate nutrients back into the soil. Birds, children and even adults enjoy a rummage through them. Leaves respond to their own world, their size determined by the amount of sun or shade. Silently, I wonder how many millions of them fall in the estate in the average autumn, happily deciding against any attempt at counting them. Daylight is ebbing away, but the leaves are a welcome radiant splash in the dark months and a reminder that after this final burst of colour, winter is just around the corner. Thinking of their numbers calls to mind Derek Mahon's remarkable poem 'Leaves': 'Somewhere there is an afterlife / Of dead leaves, / A forest filled with an infinite / Rustling and sighing.'

Winter

'The first fall of snow is not only an event, but it is a magical event. You go to bed in one kind of world and wake up to find yourself in another quite different world, and if this is not an enchantment, then where is it to be found?'

J.B. Priestley, *Apes and Angels*

'That you have such a February face / So full of frost, of storm, and cloudiness?'

William Shakespeare, *Much Ado About Nothing*

The smell of early December and damp earth brings with it freezing weather, a taste of frost and supercharged moisture in the air. In parts of County Down they call this a 'dreich' morning where a dank mist lingers, accompanied by a steady mizzle – or drizzle – of rain lasting several hours. A Scottish word, it also means 'tedious' or 'monotonous', echoing the weather this particular Friday: grey and gloomy, with uninviting low temperatures.

For several weeks I have collected twigs and branches that have fallen to the ground, drying them in a basket to use on the open fire. It feels like a perfect day to enjoy Montalto firecrackers in the living room. The flames ignite quickly with the crackle of kindling sticks, sizzling and spitting. They give off immediate heat, producing showers of sparks, a few jumping out onto the rug. The fireguard prevents any further sparks a-leaping, and I add the chopped hardwoods of beech, oak and ash. I bought them from the log-men who reckon they are the best burners. It is an organic time of year and it is hypnotising to watch the flames dancing around the burning wood, bringing an animated glow to the hearth. It feels curiously like reaching back into prehistory, an evocative connection with our ancestors through the act of burning parts of a real tree inside and managing not to set the living room on fire.

Once vigorously established, a shovelful of coal generates more heat. Another method of bringing about internal heat involves pouring myself a blended hot malt whisky. To add to the Scottish link, I delve into Norman MacCaig's *Collected Poems*. The writer, who was born in Edinburgh, is renowned for the skill of his supremely accessible nature poetry, and an hour spent in his company brings *joie de vivre*. His short simple poems of exactitude are playful, lyrical and versatile, and make fun of themselves. Their author, who had an exuberant imagination, wrote original, thought-provoking work. MacCaig's poems are about nature, birds and landscape, highlighting Assynt in north-west Scotland. His nickname was 'Two fags' MacCaig. Someone once asked how long it took him to write a poem and he replied, 'Two fags.' He was photographed with a fag at each corner of his mouth and liked to say, 'One for each lung.' MacCaig lived to be eighty-five, writing over 4,000 poems but destroying 2,800 of them as not being good enough. Seamus Heaney, an admirer, once said, 'He means poetry to me.' His poems are like a lively shot of espresso or, in my case, a tot of Isle of Skye whisky.

Suitably fortified with words and heat to combat the plummeting temperatures, and having banked up the fire with slack, I set out with a heavy brush to sweep up leaves on the path around the cottage, turning up seeds and nuts and disturbing tiny creatures of the soil and undergrowth. A mini flurry of activity comes from the *ziida-ziida* notes of a solitary goldcrest and from the jubilant call of wrens. Although I cannot see either of them, I am astonished that such small birds can survive in sub-zero temperatures. They appear to like being close to other birds for mutual body warmth and are looking for insects, although there are few of those around. While filling the bin, I pause to inspect a spider swinging on a breeze using silky threads known as gossamer (abbreviated from the Middle-English 'goose-summer' and referring to early winter). Sweeping the leaves seems like a pointless exercise, but engaging in the task offers an unforgettable moment of small wonder brightening a dark and dreary December day.

On a walk to the back entrance at the far end of the estate, a flock of cackling fieldfares – colourful thrushes from Scandinavia – plunder hawthorns, guzzling on the scarlet berries. They work their way along hedges laden with hips and haws, part of their winter larder. Without warning, the birds explode into spring-heeled flight, their backs a rich chestnut as they head off to find other pastures with their harsh *tsak-tsak* flight call.

Scratchy and high-pitched squeaky notes emanate from other parts of the woodland. As I attempt to pin down where the noise is coming from, through a jigsaw of branches beyond the lake and lawn, a movement catches my eye and through binoculars I spot a skulking blackcap, moving in a slow, deliberate manner. It is burrowing into a branch, nibbling for a few brief seconds, all the while keeping an eye out for threatening feathered unfriends. The bird, *Sylvia atricapilla*, is a warbler with a glossy black cap, black eyes, a thin white orbital ring and a long thinnish bill. The birds are passage migrants, arriving from northern or eastern Europe and their call is a repeated *tacc-tacc*. Swiftly, it flits between branches, an arboreal explorer whizzing off energetically to make forays in different trees before settling on a beech, where it is joined by the female of the species. She has a bright chestnut cap with more greyish-brown colouring. The happy couple indulge in a swirling game of 'chasies', branch-hopping, watched all the time from an elevated viewpoint by a wary magpie contemplating the everyday display of affection.

Aside from the active birds, many of the estate's animals are hunkering down for a winter inertia of controlled quiescence or slowed development. It is a dormant landscape, and in the case of some insects, it is their diapause, from the Greek *diapausis*: a period of suspended growth accompanied by decreased metabolism.

Winter gnats work through the cold months swarming in nooks, but female worker wasps spend the time in hibernation until the spring, and not a bee, hornet or flying midge is to be seen. According to the gamekeeper, badgers do not hibernate but fall into something of a catatonic trance or state of torpor, spending most of their time snoozing. Occasionally, when hunger gets the better of them, I spot them appearing out of their setts foraging for worms or small rodents.

Plants are divested of their colour and the life of the woodland centres on the ground. Each day the light dwindles to a few hours, but there is still evidence of vitality, with leaf buds appearing on trees, some of which show patterns and textures in a palette of colours visible only at this time of year. One such tree is the deciduous common birch, which, without its leaves, has a butter-smooth, creamy-coloured bark now more clearly seen. In Celtic mythology, birch is a tree of beginnings, symbolising renewal and purification; ecologists refer to it as a pioneer species – the first to colonise newly created habitats. Nearby, a large horse chestnut tree, which looks eminently suitable for climbing, has produced dark reddish-brown and sticky buds, while the beeches have grown long, narrow, sharp-pointed buds with papery scales. Oak buds are small and brown, with a cluster at the tip of the shoots. Along the main pathway into the estate, lime trees sprout crimson buds with two scales of distinct size. A few months earlier, they were dappled with light-brown winged seeds. In another grove, branches of old willows are coated with yellow and green lichens.

By the winter solstice, the elusive sun has stalled on the shortest day and longest night. Solstice, appropriately from the Latin *sol* and *sistere*, means 'to stand still'. There is little sign of it now until the run into the festive season and the year's turning, or 'the turn of the day', as it is known here. My afternoon yuletide walk is completed in gathering dusk to a background of avian roosting rituals, a round of ultra-quiet cheeps, and a few desultory chirps of the house sparrow while the wind shivers through the trees. In these end-of-year moments daylight lasts just a few hours, ending around 3.15 p.m., but each morning it begins to inch forward a little earlier. It is a sign of rebirth, the beginning of a new solar year, the sun rising again, and every day edging higher in the sky, bringing with it the spring and a revival of growth and opportunity. Winter lets in the light and there is a subtle enchantment to the wood with few of nature's alarm calls. There is a breathless quality to the air and a stark beauty in the bare branches. A jackdaw, its head cocked, watches something intently, vigilant and motionless, like a king of his own castle. From a thick tangle of bushes, a robin delivers a sharp, silvery burst of song, characteristic of woodland at the tail end of the year. As passerines, robins are drawn to perches, such as a bin or a spade, and from these, with sharp eyesight, they survey the ground for insects, indulging in a swift perch-and-pounce process.

We swoop upon the greenery surrounding our doorstep and make a traditional holly wreath to hang on the front door. Holly is known as 'The Lord of the Waning Year'. Ours is a curious mixture of prickly, sharp leaves and twigs, combined with ivy, pinecones, a few evergreen garden shrubs and conifer sprigs, with a seasoning of scarlet berries and fallen leaves thrown in for good measure – the whole decorated with a red ribbon tied in a bow and a mini dangling ornamental snowman. The departing log-men wave from their van as they drive off for their seasonal break: 'Go well and be blessed.' We are, and we celebrate the bleak midwinter with a glass of punch while listening to the contact calls of unseen birds.

After Christmas the first cold snap arrives. In the lethargic and gloomy period before the New Year, the estate looks as if it has been showered with icing sugar. We warm up with hot drinks in the nearby Century Bar before returning to our bitterly cold cottage, which suffers from a lack of double glazing, and without the warmth of a burning fire does not stay warm for long. Ice crystals appear on the inside of the windows with jewel-like patterns forming shapes resembling rosettes. Trees, plants and hedges draped in ghostly white cobwebs look as though they have been sprayed with a powder. This rime is created by a damp icy wind blowing over plants and branches, and by cool water droplets that have frozen almost immediately and turned into frost.

***

A New Year's day bustle, with birds whizzing and skittering in all directions, enlivens the woods. A magpie uses its beak to shovel leaves to one side in a serious quest for food. Two riders on chestnut horses canter past on their way through the grounds to join a hunt. Their clippety-clop ignites a quartet of blue tits, chasing through the trees with their liquid trill, like miniature fighter pilots in aerial warfare. In a late afternoon mooch there is an unsettled feel to the air, with a twisting theatre of dark clouds and a couple of rambunctious thunderclaps, leading us to beat a hasty retreat indoors. We wake the next day to a heavy frost that has crystallised our world. It is a day for scarves, hats, heavy boots and frozen fingers as our gloves cannot be found. Icy wind tingles my skin and stings my eyes with wind-tickling tears. Magical crystals of six-sided frost have formed on water that was left in buckets, and on the car windscreen. Frost has crisped the normally manicured green lawn and the lake has frozen into an ice rink, while paths are slippery. High above, the sky is an anti-freeze blue.

In the depths of winter most animals are indoors, snuggled up in their burrows, nests, hides and dreys for comfort and warmth. On his rounds, the groundsman says that an early frost can sometimes help break up heavy soil, but it also kills weeds and reduces the pest population. Small, fascinating aspects of sylvan life catch my attention. The frost has turned intricately created spider webs into thin necklaces slung between branches on shrubs. On the forest floor, leaves are rigid-stiff, while across the grass, the slender and frozen blades have a magical quality. Spiders have spun delicate snares on the leaves creating tiny dew droplets, known as 'dewfall'. In Greek mythology, Ersa is the goddess and personification of dew. According to the myth, the dew in the morning was created when Eos (Ersa's aunt), goddess of the dawn, cried for her son's death, although later he received immortality.

By 11.30 a.m. the sun makes an appearance as a perfectly formed orb of whiteness, framed as a striking sight between lofty trees. Slowly it rises with a halo into a haze of brightness that is hard to look at for any length of time, giving off a strange orange hue. Within a few minutes it returns to its white aura, set amidst a thin veil of wispy clouds in a silent silver-pewter sky. The frost lingers for the morning, clearing in the early afternoon before it is replaced by a thick fog enveloping the estate. The fog creates an atmospheric mood, a magical mist known in Irish mythology as the *féth fíada*. The ancient supernatural race, the Tuatha Dé Danann, conjured up the veil to hide from humans. On the path in front of me, far from hiding, a tiny shivery wren, with its up-tilted tail and jerky movements, is uncertain which way to proceed since visibility is limited. I have often been bemused by the fact that one of the smallest species in the birding world, and with the shortest name, is known as 'The King of the Birds' because of its assumed cleverness. The wise bird is said to have outsmarted the eagle in a competition to see who could fly higher. The wren is venerated in Irish mythology and celebrated in rural areas where festivals are held on St Stephen's/Boxing Day.

Next morning, after a quiet but heavy fall in the dead of the night, we open the curtains to reveal the ground gripped in a thick layer of snow, a new world of sharp wonders. There is a stillness, and a golden, enigmatic quality to the light that makes it feel good to be alive in this temporarily repainted white landscape. I recall the words of Robert Graves from his short but sublime poem 'Like Snow': 'She, then, like snow in a dark night, / Fell secretly. And the world waked / With dazzling of the drowsy eye, / So that some muttered 'Too much light', / And drew the curtains close.' Winter has arrived, not so much with a feminine vengeance, but more a satisfactory feeling of the scene-shifting of nature and a sense of otherworldliness. The appearance of the demesne has changed, obliterating familiars and blurring distinctions. Trees, in soundless wedding-dress white, have taken an unusual shape, their branches heavy with the burden of snow. The farm shed beside our cottage is whited out, while a pristine duvet of milk-white airbrushes tarmacked paths.

The snow, which is about four inches deep, brings a fresh play of light and a new dimension of awareness, especially of footprints. There is something exhilarating about being the first person to enjoy a soft and silent walk over the snow, admiring how the greenery has vanished. Winter's chill, however, is not much fun for the birds and presents a challenging time. They are adapting to a constantly changing environment in which food sources, as well

J.W. Carey's stylish painting of Montalto house and lake, *circa* 1890s.

'The Battle of Ballynahinch', 13 June 1798, oil painting by Thomas Robinson. The original painting hangs in Áras an Uachtaráin, Phoenix Park, Dublin. (Courtesy of the Office of the President)

A bird's-eye view reveals the scale of the 400-acre estate, but not its mysteries.
(© Trevor Ferris)

One of Montalto's ancient trees, the giant redwood sequoia, with its spongy
bark, flourishes in an embankment close to the main house.
(© Trevor Ferris)

The small summer house captured in winter between oak trees. Summer houses were originally designed to provide shade from the heat of the sun. (Courtesy of Montalto Estate)

The speckled wood is one of the more common butterflies found in the grounds. It perches in sunny spots, enjoying blackberries, then spirals into the air. (© Trevor Ferris)

Montalto lake and Winter Garden. The lake was designed in the shape of a fish, and is home to waterfowl such as wigeon, coots, teal, mute swans, and crested and little grebes. (© Trevor Ferris)

The remains of the spine wall in the Lost Garden, which originally divided the glasshouse from the boiler house and potting shed, a relic of an earlier horticultural time. (© Trevor Ferris)

as water and shelter, are severely limited, and smaller creatures may not survive. There must be a sense of wonderment as to why the ground beneath them has turned from a green sward to a white-out. In the case of voles and mice, however, which live underground, they can survive happily under snow for weeks on end in a maze of tunnels.

A walk along undisturbed paths shows that woodland mammals have ventured out. Slowly, and with head down, I search the ground carefully, trying to read the prints of birds and mammals, to rewind time to see where they came from and where they have disappeared to. The wavy tracks of partridges are large three-toed prints that reach a sudden end, giving rise to more questions than answers. Other birds have indulged in the spectacle, leaving their imprints in the snow running in all directions at the front and back of the cottage and along paths in a random manner. Tracks appear to criss-cross, or to stop abruptly, leading to a guessing game, while a few have gone off-piste. They may represent a brisk dash to a regular destination, a stand-off with a rival or a brief flurry from the nests to search for food before heading undercover again. Some prints run in a straight line, while others zig and zag. On a closer look, I make out the pawprints of a hare. Farther along on a path beside the lawn are the giveaway signs of magpies dragging their long tails, generating an identifiable fine line in the snow.

There are also unreadable patterns, and it is hard to detect from the infinitely varied small shapes and sizes of spoors or runes which animals they belong to. I come across the large front and smaller hind pawprints of squirrels at the base of pine trees. The creature's track is neat, with two pairs of footprints, the hind ones close together while the front ones are parallel but wider apart. I make out the footmarks of a fox, single prints in a straight line, which follow the same route as the birds and could be regular paths taken each morning. At one point a hare jumps up disturbing the snow from brambles and setting off at breakneck speed through the trees. There is evidence that wood pigeons, who are accustomed to surviving lower temperatures with their downy fluff for insulation, frequent this grove. Along the main paths no tyre tracks cross the snow, but slowly I make boot impressions with my size eight feet.

The tracks represent a parallel world whose inhabitants in normal weather go to great lengths to keep their activities hidden, leaving no trace of their shiftings and stirrings. Following the ground movements of small creatures is impossible for most of the year. Animal tracking through prints in the snow is an entire field of scientific study and a subject providing endless hours of fascination and speculation. Tracks are divided into three groups: sole walkers are the animals that walk on the flat of the foot; toe walkers are cats and dogs; nail walkers represent the ungulates covering horses, deer, pigs, cows and goats – the only one found in the demesne being horses. In his book on the peregrine, J.A. Baker notes that footprints in the snow are strangely moving: 'They seem an almost shameful betrayal of the creatures that make them, as though something of themselves had been left defenceless.'

A jackdaw *chacks* through the stillness and a blackbird appears out of nowhere, searching the hard, snowy grass in a futile quest for worms, while a sparrow flutters in and out of a hedge. A hooded crow weaves its way across the sky, bemused by the new colour facet.

The dilatory sun produces a glistening sheen on shrubs and hedges, just off the path that runs in front of the cottage. The snow enhances the grounds, lending them a special enchantment. It also leads to reminiscence of heavy snowfalls in childhood winters, snowballing, tobogganing and building large snowmen. The very word 'snow' conjures up ephemeral snapshots of elation, exhilaration and excitement, anticipation and possibility, but also uncertainty, with questions for the grown-ups: 'Will there be more snow soon? How long will it last? Will school remain closed?' From an early age I was a confirmed chionophile (from the Greek word *chion*, meaning snow), and so it creates a powerful recollection of the delight and tumbling fun of snowball fights with the right kind of firm and crisp packing. Building snowmen involved a search for stones or large lumps of black coal, to be inserted as eye decorations, and a carrot for the nose. We had all the paraphernalia of duffel coats, gloves, hats, scarves, wellington boots and two pairs of thick socks. Crucially, it also meant days off school, since no buses were running and few cars ventured out on the ice-covered roads. Clearing a path for the postman or milkman and shovelling the hard-packed snow into piles of mini mountains was fun and went hand in hand with slip-sliding.

Sometimes I wonder about the memory playing tricks, and if the winters of long ago were much worse than the present. They seem to have been more severe in childhood when snowploughs and gritters were prevalent, compared to adult life. One January that I recall – having just started primary school – was in 1963. Heavy snow fell across the eastern and northern parts of Ireland, making it one of the coldest winters on record, bringing blizzards and exceptionally low temperatures. Thousands were cut off by snowdrifts, while rivers and lakes turned solid and water pipes froze in houses.

The winter finery transforms the Montalto woodland, while the big house all by itself looks more impressive than normal, a romantic Christmas card scene set against a pure white backdrop. I think back much further in time mulling over the various roles the estate has had, the historic parts it has played and the tempestuous weathers it has witnessed in more than two centuries.

The rise and fall of the winter wind forces me back to the present and is something that I have come to fear, but few other sounds break the bloated silence. When it calms, the wind is a subtle stirring, moving across the grass, scattering seeds from tall lime trees. At other times it borders on a murmur, accompanied by hums, creaks and squeaks. It is formless, almost invisible, or at most a plaintive whistle, rippling through the crowns of beech, firs and oaks.

More snowflakes start to flutter, soft and damp, blanketing any noise, but they are not on the scale of the overnight fall; these are more insubstantial, coming under the delightful name 'flindrikin', heard in parts of north-east Ireland and in Scotland. Each snowflake is a marvel of design. Henry David Thoreau, who enjoyed walking through snow in the Walden woods, wrote that he 'could not feel more wonder if a star fell and landed on his coat'. While the frost enlivens the air with a bitter chilliness, the snow brings a serenity. I disappear back indoors to escape the freezing temperatures, and curl up on the warmth of my settee dipping into Robert Frost's 'Desert Places': 'Snow falling and night falling fast, oh, fast / In a field I looked into going past, / And the ground almost covered smooth in snow, / But a few weeds and stubble showing last. / The woods around it have it – it is theirs. / All animals are smothered in their lairs. / I am too absent-spirited to count; / The loneliness includes me unawares.'

After the snow turns to slush, a thaw sets in. The Janus-faced month, named in honour of a Roman god, is a time that bestrides winter, bringing an ominous change in the atmosphere. Most evenings give way to a heavy breeze, gradually gaining momentum and developing strength. On occasion it is no more than a capricious gasp or gentle groan, but at other times it sounds like a shriek or screech, reverberating through the woods. I become accustomed to getting out of bed, pulling back the curtains, observing the trees swaying heavily with their crowns flailing, but never becoming complacent about them. Sometimes we feared the worst – a tree falling on the cottage, smashing down on the nearby sheds or falling to the ground around us. The temperature has dropped to minus four degrees Celsius, and the cold becomes more numbing each night. The invigorating wind has many personas in its symphonic make up. It is turning nasty, and turmoil in the stratosphere is on the way.

It is the first Saturday in grey-grim January and the end of a tempestuous wind-filled week. All evening the enigmatic 'Montalto Roarer', as we labelled it, has been whipping up, realising our fears. These were the days before most storms were imbued with names which somehow belittle their devastating nature. The 'Roarer' has a character of its own. The fifth consecutive stormy night is underway, gathering more whirling energy each evening. The forecast on the radio warns that it will reach gale-force or beyond, and tonight it hurtles into overdrive. By 11 p.m. it is barrelling headlong across the drumlin countryside into the estate.

Throughout the night the merciless wind, with barely any respite, roars, whistles and howls in all directions around the cottage doors, moaning down the chimney, testing the foundations. Windows rattle with an alarming intensity. The accompanying eerie moans and groans are unnerving, yet at the same time exhilarating, if disquieting, and make it hard to sleep. Around 3 a.m., after considerable tossing and turning, I rise and peer out at younger trees thrashing and swishing around, as though trying to make good their escape from the ground, and I ponder the fate of the bigger ones.

On Sunday morning the extent of the devastating tantrum is apparent. One of the biggest and noblest beeches in the estate, a tree of enormous dimensions, came crashing down on the main circular drive near the front of the big house. The tree had lorded it over the lawn and lake, and frequently on my way past I had admired its changing colour patterns, moving from brilliant yellow to rich, reddish-brown mahogany. Young newly planted trees have been uprooted and ripped from their shallow grip, now sagging limply, while hefty branches have come off others. But they do not have the pedigree and powerful sense of longevity of their venerable neighbour, and their loss is less profound. The fall of an ancient tree is a sad occasion. It marks the death of a living monument, a touchstone that has been a shared source of happiness to a vast universe of organisms linked to a multicellular life of interconnectivity. I reflect on the food chains the tree hosted and the fact that over the decades it gave nourishment, sheltering thousands of nesting birds, while mosses and lichen clothed its bark.

The beech tree, over eighty feet tall and more than two centuries old, was wrenched out of the ground with prodigious force leaving a gaping and disturbing hole. It had been weak for several years and its immense root network had rotted. Holes in the trunk were attacked by algae and opportunistic fungi, as well as a multitude of leaf-guzzling insects. Nevertheless, hefting such an enormous body out of the ground after 200 years' imprisonment is a major achievement and illustrates how tenuous a grip it had on the earth after all the decades of growth. Now lying spreadeagled, smelling of resin, birds descend on it for a Sunday morning breakfast, scampering round its bulbous trunk, gorging on its girth, fluttering and leaping about in the branches splintered across its exposed remains. They are all atwitter with the loss of a tree that had been both a hospitable host and stalwart friend, but is now lifeless, a grotesque sight, its innards, roots and filaments on display. A blackbird fossicks through thick dark-green foliage and brown leaf litter, hoping to find insects and spiders, before turning its attention to scratching noisily at leaves on branches. Gnats emerge dancing across the doomed carcass, joined by scuttling bark beetles inspecting the wreckage with forensic diligence before enjoying a buffet. On one thick branch a column of wood ants is on the march. Creepy-crawlies swarm around a dazzlingly white previously unseen section of the bark.

Nervously, a jittery magpie circles down, hunkering on the lawn before exploring. A second one joins in and, living up to their nickname 'chatter-pies', they gossip in conspiratorial conversation about the veteran tree's demise, their long black tails wagging nineteen-to-the-dozen. The fall of the beech has left a gap in the tree-wall like a missing tooth, but the other trees around the lake are strangely reposeful. Mangled wreckage lies across the path, blocking any traffic, although there is none on this Sunday morning. The jagged edges of several huge branches are reminiscent of a sharp rocky outcrop in the mountains. The groundsman appears, along with two local men, and I help sweep up leaves. A chainsaw, like an electric guitar, struggles through some chords and performs the last rites, cutting parts of the contorted trunk into manageable logs for firewood in local hearths. The men, 'tree mourners', are saddened by the death of a tree of such stature and one with which they had a remarkable kinship. One of them says a number of country roads are blocked with fallen trees and so closed to traffic.

The groundsman has a profound feeling for stricken trees and plants, and has seen many of the beech's neighbours collapse, but this tree had outlived them all. It was one of the oldest on the estate and the epitome of forest grace. He grieves for it as an old friend. It was here a long time before he came. 'We thought that tree was immortal, but old beeches are particularly susceptible to storms as the roots often don't penetrate deeply.'

It would surprise many that the beech arrived in Ireland relatively recently, approximately 500 years ago. Beech has since naturalised itself, becoming, as in the case of Montalto, a mainstay of many Irish forests, woodlands and hedges. It keeps its lower branches clad in skirts of leaves that fan down to the ground while other trees concentrate their leaves only on their canopy. Tree lovers admire their sweeping shape, smooth bark, and especially the colour of their leaves in the spring, as well as their golden ducats in the autumn.

In the arboreal hierarchy, the beech is one of the groundsman's favourite trees. He also likes the tall Scots pines, especially on the hill at Ednavady. 'The bark goes a rusty copper red. They are flat-topped with a flat crown and a conical appearance. The old ones are bald all the way up with a flat crown. They are handsome trees that look better as they get older and mature with age. But for all their beauty I'd still rank the beech as my all-time favourite.'

Light flecks of snow start to fall. Crows cross the lawn quietly. We look up at the sky where stately cumulus clouds hang overhead moving slowly. Two buzzards spool out of the woods. Word comes through of spectacularly destructive damage in other parts of the grounds with further tree mortality. A man pulls up in a Land Rover, saying that many young trees have been uprooted in a conifer plantation. Other beeches are also casualties, at Mill Bridge and in the Low Wood. In some areas huge branches have fallen to the ground, snapped by the storm. Roofs have been damaged in stone buildings and wooden fences felled. All around, the debris created by the cruel hand of nature in the dead of a winter's night is a depressing spectacle. There is a palpable sense of bereavement in the January stillness, and it is a sobering sight. The groundsman grabs sackfuls of branches, jumps into the jeep and heads off to check on the Low Wood.

After he has gone, I think about the longevity of *Fagus sylvatica*, about the numerous seen and unseen dramas enacted inside it, the vast and complex whirl of life which revolved around it, the animals under its protection and about its spirit. Nobody could start to imagine what the tree had witnessed and endured during its lifetime. Planted as a status symbol around the late eighteenth century, it has shed millions of leaves and leaf buds, been visited for fodder by hundreds of thousands of termites, ants, bees, moths, micromoths and butterflies, and lived through tens of thousands of moons and sunsets. It withstood the Night of the Big Wind in January 1839 and the violent storm-cyclone of October 1987. It competed for water, light and space, survived freezing nights and hot days, as well as countless storms.

For centuries the tree was a feed-station of infinite beauty and complexity. It may have hosted a secret threadlike network of fungal mycelium, while up to 100 species could have benefited from it. Generations of centipedes and millipedes, worms, aphids, leaf beetles and weevils, ladybirds, snails, spiders, woodlice, slugs and bugs, and an army of other insects derived comfort and shelter from it, gnawing its roots. Mice and squirrels gobbled up its beechmast, the edible nuts of the beech lying on the ground. It provided protein and enriched the lives of a litany of varied species, who flirted with it and perched on its branches for social gatherings. How many crevices, nesting holes and roosts it harboured is anyone's guess; its bole has been sniffed, its resin tasted, its bark hugged, branches climbed and leaves kissed. The tree may be dead but it is still providing fodder for nutrients, and I feel a warm glow about knowing a few of its secrets. From the skirl of the mistle thrush to the fluting notes of the blackbird, it played host to the calls of countless songbirds, while its branches were a perch for dynasties of wood pigeons. Visited by many, loved by all, it was an ecological megalopolis. How the mighty city has fallen.

The power of the storm has shaken birdlife. Its violent beauty may have wreaked havoc, but it has also released a mysterious energy. Around the grounds multiple wounds are visible to trees, with fractured or bent trunks spanning the width of the driveway. It resembles a silent battlefield. Hefty limbs have snapped, hanging limply with dazzlingly light wood interiors. A towering thin pine tilts at a more dangerous-looking angle than the Leaning Tower of Pisa. Overhanging sycamores show evidence of decay or fungus, which speeds up the damage, most beyond repair. Arboreal litter is everywhere. Paths are strewn with the wreckage of hundreds of storm-beaten branches and twigs bent into ungainly patterns, shapes or sizes like something found in a decorative metalwork exhibition but useful for winter fuel. A line from Robert Frost's 'Birches' springs to mind: 'Such heaps of broken glass to sweep away / You'd think the inner dome of heaven had fallen.'

There is a sharp crackle when I trample on the twigs, making them more manageable to carry. Leaves are scattered across the floor, while chunky coffee-coloured globular pinecones and desiccated needles lie at forlorn angles, another victim of the storm. They are from a tall Atlas cedar tree, *Cedrus atlantica*, a coniferous evergreen in the pine family. With spiral scales and bracts arranged around a central axis, they appear in assorted peculiarities of individual sizes up to nine inches long, some shaped like a banana, while others are cylindrical. There is a belief that cones are a symbol of human enlightenment, resurrection, eternal life and regeneration. They are also said to symbolise the promise of spring and rebirth. The conifer cones are light and have a soft, crunchy feel, while the spruce ones are quiet and squidgy. I recall a short mnemonic to help identify needles: Fat, Friendly Fir; Plural, Pokey Pine; and Sharp, Spiral Spruce.

After such a stormy night, the fallen beech tree offers a haven for insects. The bird silence represents part of the quiet dank character of the season and is broken by the foresters slicing up trunks with a chainsaw. Nonetheless, by 13 January, St Hilary's Day – traditionally the coldest day of the year in the folklore calendar – the birds are animated. A clamour of swarthy rooks is cawing gutturally. Robins are one of the few birds to sing their ultra-early spring song, and although it is intermittent, it warns other males to keep out of the owner's territory. Their bellicosity lasts the year round and as each day passes their song becomes more robust.

The next day, 14 January, is my birthday. In parts of France the date is known as the 'Feast of the Ass', a religious ceremony involving donkeys. It is believed to celebrate the biblical post-Christmas Flight into Egypt, to which the animal was traditionally central. As a Capricorn, I am a child of winter. We are more noted for our connection to mountain goats than donkeys, and sometimes the goat comes with the tail of a fish, which makes us a strange marine-goat hybrid. We also like to think of ourselves as perfectionists, being hardworking and organised. Other common traits are ambition, discipline and self-criticism – in my case, I often wonder where it all went wrong.

That night I stare at the sky, beyond tall trees, to see if there is any sign of Beta Capricorni, the second brightest star in the Capricornus Constellation, but it is simply a mass of cloudy greyness. There is, I guess, a dark and pessimistic side to Capricorns. At the end of another birthday, with the persistent wind howling in my ears, I inform my journal that 'middle-youth' – the period from thirty to forty years of age – is gradually slipping away. Never mind perfection, it is a time for reflection, and I muse over my notes about why I have come to the woods: to feel the power of the wind, experience the humbling weather and the force of nature, connect with birdlife, escape urban noise and pollution, contemplate the night sky scattered with stars, if the empyrean allows, and rinse the city's dust from my brain.

It is, of course, Ireland's fate to be perched on the outer extremity of north-west Europe, which means it receives the full force of the Atlantic's fury. The western side of the country is worst afflicted and acts like a barrier, before the gales move across country to the east. Buckets of rain, raw winds and grey skies are an elemental feature of life. Figures show that the west of Ireland receives an average of 225 days of rainfall a year compared to the east of the country's 150 days.

Lightning flashes and thunderstorms with hail the size of table tennis balls batter the estate the next morning. It is a time for the indoors and reading, followed by two days of non-stop downpour, making a trip outside not worth considering. By the middle of the week, I complain in an alliterative fashion to my journal that I was experiencing 'one of the worst, wettest and windiest winter Wednesdays imaginable'. Eventually the rain ceases, and on a Thursday-afternoon stroll the milder air relieves the cold, as great tits break their winter silence with a piercing two-note song. I listen carefully to the serenade, one that dominates the woodland soundscape, which involves the males seeking out a partner. Several sightings of the bird reveal that it is living up to its nickname, 'black-headed bob'.

***

With the arrival of fickle February, there are around three minutes of extra light each day. Soon the days grow appreciably longer and the nights become shorter. These precious minutes of light in late afternoon are known as 'cock steps' and are said to be comparable to the stride of a male chicken. And early February signifies two important dates in the calendar. The first is St Brigid's Day (1 February), also known as Imbolc, the ancient Celtic folk tradition and festival when the prospects of spring are celebrated, and which represents a stepping stone between the seasons. As the sun creeps slightly higher in the sky, it is symbolic of hope and renewal. According to legend, it was also on this day that the Cailleach, the goddess of winter or hag woman, gathered her firewood for the rest of the winter. If she wanted winter to last longer, she would make the weather sunny, but if the conditions were bad, then the Cailleach was asleep and winter was almost over.

As if in acknowledgement of this, throughout the grounds the birds are calling from tree to tree, the unrelenting pin-sharp *tink-tink-tink* a reminder that the year is on the turn. From the branch of a tree, a song thrush pierces the air, belting out its clear and sweet fluting notes which carry across the woodland. With its buff-coloured back and creamy-brown freckled breast, its vigorous music brings a cheeriness to the start of February. The winter solstice is well behind us and the early stirrings are a sign of spring; even though animals are still hibernating, brighter days lie ahead.

Bride is celebrated as the ancient goddess of fire. In Christian times she was canonised as St Brigid and is Ireland's only female patron saint. Our ancestors believed that on the eve of her feast day she travelled through the country giving blessings and protection to homes and farms where crosses were hung in her honour. And it was on this date that prognostications of the weather were made from animals, as an old Gaelic poem recounts: 'The serpent will come from the hole/ On the brown Day of Bride, / Though there should be three feet of snow / On the flat surface of the ground.'

The second significant day is Candlemas Day (2 February), when candles were lit in parts of Ireland to celebrate the return of daylight. It was also a time for predicting the weather for the coming weeks and months, and is a reminder of a rhyme from schooldays: 'If Candlemas be fair and bright, winter will have another flight; / If Candlemas Day be clouds and rain, winter be gone and will not come again.'

Early February signals the halfway point between the winter solstice and the spring equinox. This particular Candlemas Day coincides with the arrival of a scattering of snowdrops, known under their folk name 'Fair Maids of February', glinting in the sunshine. Some are in plain sight in a tight cluster of up to twenty, with their signature white petals, while others are partly hidden under leaves in a quiet corner of a shaded grove, their hoods drooping. The first part of their botanical name, *Galanthus nivalis*, derives from a combination of the Greek words for milk (*gala*) and flower (*anthus*). The snowdrops' appearance bodes well for fresh life in the estate, where I detect the air has a softer feel with a faint honey scent coming from them. But the 'Fair Maids' are fleeting and will disappear within a few weeks. They are best regarded as a seasonal starting pistol and an early feast for bees, soon to be followed by more colourful blooms. Growing beside them in semi-shade, I discover clumps of the shiny yellow flowering winter aconite, also known as monkshood, symbolising new beginnings. Elsewhere grasses and hedges still maintain a craggy look, in need of a sustained burst of sunshine. But the cold snap has helped trigger germination, encouraging plants to flourish as part of a process called vernalisation.

Although the air of early February remains layered with a chill, the morning rush hour is on the move and animal life has stepped up a gear. Right outside our front door, birds are zipping with an urgency so fast that binoculars are useless. On short sallies, back and forth, they fetch sticks or carry twigs in their bills as part of a nest-building spree, shoring them up, adding comfort and warmth. Few of them perch or sit still. Everywhere there is constant traffic of high-speed aerial displays, while a repertoire of frantic shrieks and squeaks, urgent chuckles and clicks, short two-note blasts, and a raft of elongated tinkling provides a stream of surround-sound. It is astonishing that they avoid colliding, and strange how they manage such synchronised manoeuvres. The birds' body clocks have tracked the new light, triggering the release of buzzing sex hormones, a prelude to breeding. They are now indulging in melodic notes, and while a few are hesitant, others have lost the run of themselves and their vocal cords. However, although the birds are limbering up and in training for the spring, they seem agitated.

The new light may not be razor sharp, but just before the deciduous trees with their barren outstretched branches come into leaf, it is the strongest that the birds have seen since autumn and has put them on edge by making them more visible. I scan the trees and bushes with my naked eye. With their long yellow bill and light speckling, the starlings are restless, while two pied wagtails are fidgety and an uncertain blackbird reverses awkwardly up a hedge, resulting in a hissy fit. The sustained sharp burst of activity lasts for less than fifteen minutes, and in that time I note the birds' flight paths: wavy, zigzag, undulating and purposeful – while a kestrel with all the dexterity of a fighter pilot, swoops its way through the high branches, hovering for a few seconds, which may explain the other birds' hue and cry. High up, they screech nonsense, while others release a wolf whistle ending with a yelp or vociferous call. A sinister party of hooded crows arrives on the grass, spoiling for a fight. In the vegetation around the lake's edge, the churr from mistle thrushes rings out across the placid water. These birds were once called stormcocks, and are known, according to my dictionary of collective nouns, as 'a mutation'.

The Battle of Ballynahinch may have been fought in 1798, but something menacing is now afoot, with bird wars being enacted in mini-dramas. A brouhaha breaks out between rooks in a treetop, which in turn sets off a fracas among crows. From several different branches, four crows, keen to pick a fight, hold a clamorous conversation with those on the ground. Two on the forest floor thrash their wings, yelling up to them like bickering neighbours and waiting for a staggered response. Suddenly they fly up, angular and aggressive, swing around and swoop back to the ground. It is hard to make out the cause of their angst – perhaps a row over renovating a nest – but a specific incident sparks off a frenzied squawking contretemps. Known in Scotland as a 'stramash', it is referred to by Gaelic football commentators in Ireland as a 'shemozzle'.

From mid-February, an encouraging sign that spring is on the way is the brisk song of the chaffinch. The bird specialises in a long rapid run of *chip-chip-chip* notes ending in a flourish. A bitter wind persists for several days, but there is a clarity that is intrinsic in the winter. On a late afternoon walk, oddly-shaped holes in the ground where soil has been disturbed are evidence of unknown creatures at work – part of the mystery of woodland life in unexplored territory. The next couple of weeks see a considerable amount of pair bonding and flirting between the birds. The blackbird delivers a *chuck-chuck* call, while robins flick their wings, and the humble sparrows tune up for the mating season. There is an anxiety about the sparrows that alight quickly on the end of a branch, craning their necks with an air of detachment. Within a few seconds they are gone, leaving a quivering branch behind.

On a morning of low winter sun that rises to a brightness, known as apricity since it is giving off meagre warmth, large clouds of tiny flies swirl rapidly over the lawn up to ten feet above the grass. As if on a string, they bob vertically and are within touching distance of each other. The winter gloom is lifting and I shade the sun with my arm and, with binoculars, try to catch them in sharp focus, but they refuse to remain static. The rare shafts of sunlight have animated them, bringing hope of warmer months and the end of short-lived days. Around a compost heap, gnats circle en bloc, indulging in a tête-à-tête, as their numbers gradually dwindle, while others spiral steadily like a yo-yo, twisting and turning.

In late February the consoling factor is that no matter what the weather, the lustre of the days ahead will see the sun rising higher in the sky. At the start of the last week of the month my ears ring with the energy of penetrating birdsong. Cycling around the estate gives me an overview of the bird noise, which includes the almost human-sounding soft whistle of a bullfinch. The rest constitute an audio mix of wheezing and barking, harsher nasal calls, excitable and alarm-filled crescendos and repeated diminuendos. Frequently there is a cold snap at the end of February, and legend states that the final nights of the month are known as the 'steel nights' since the chill cuts so deep. In the Roman Rite, the Throne of the Chair of Saint Peter – a relic conserved in St Peter's Basilica in the Vatican City – is celebrated on 22 February. While Roman martyrology assigns 29 June as the actual feast day of both Peter and Paul, the Feast of the Chair of Saint Peter on its February date warns that 'If cold at St Peter's Day, it will last longer.' On this date I detect that the winter gloom is slowly withdrawing its grip as the natural mulch and leaf litter which wrapped up the wildflowers have started to clear.

My journal reflects that it had been a cold and hard period for the creatures of the estate but anticipates that in a few weeks' time there should be evidence of a weakening of winter's grip with unfurling greenery alongside flourishing plants. Although there is a flat atmosphere, tiny signals of rebirth are building incrementally, with flowers slowly awakening. Aside from the snowdrops and aconite, hardly a daisy has raised its head, and I form the impression that some plants are 'in waiting' but too shy to appear. There is, however, evidence of tangible touches of spring as the small red flowers of hazel sprout from twigs. In another neck of the woods I come across shoots of dog's mercury – an indicator of an ancient woodland – which has a poisonous reputation. Hawthorn blossom is also in flower, while elsewhere the tall spears of wild daffodils appear out of the roots. As a contrast, they are interspersed with clutches of stumpy purple and white crocuses, creating a heartwarming display, their stems remaining resolutely underground. Lying all around the forest floor, branches, twigs and debris are a reminder of the January storm and of the old warning that 'A February spring is not worth a pin', which means you should not be fooled by a bout of spring-like weather in the last days of February. The American writer Dorothy Aldis summed up this time of year in her poem 'When': 'In February there are days, / Blue, and nearly warm ... / When winter lifts a little bit / And spring peeks through the crack.'

Spring

'Ah, passing few are they who speak,
Wild stormy month! in praise of thee;
Yet, though the winds are loud and bleak,
Thou art a welcome month to me.'

William Cullen Bryant, 'March'

'A Light exists in Spring
Not present on the Year
At any other period –
When March is scarcely here.'

Emily Dickinson, 'A Light exists in Spring'

The high bleating of a frisky lamb is a cheery sound and evidence that hibernal days are behind us. Nature plays many cards and the coming of spring is a gradual process, but by the beginning of March the winds have calmed to a languorous breeze and brighter days slowly unfurl across the estate as it creaks into life after a tough winter. Early spring sunlight squints through the tops of trees and there is an intoxicating air about the light, with an anticipation of fewer storms ahead. Traditionally, March is a mix of spring warmth and wintry cold, and the month is no stranger to bitter weather and snow. It is often regarded as a transition period from winter to spring. The old saying 'March comes in like a lion and goes out like a lamb' was first popularised by the physician and historian Thomas Fuller in his 1732 compendium *Gnomologia: Adages and Proverbs.*

I step outside on 1 March, St David's Day, with a bounce in my stride and discover the animals have a spring in their step too. Many have emerged from their winter hideaways to inspect the weather and the bio-abundance of life becoming apparent. In the meteorologists' calendar it is now said to be spring, and the estate is a microcosmic ecosystem that is immeasurable. Birch trees are showing off small triangular shiny leaves glinting like emeralds in the sunlight. A wood pigeon struts among the plants, pausing every so often to sniff. Quiet and alone, I sit with a flask of tomato soup beside a fence-post at a small woodland plantation at one end of the estate overlooking fields. I have been told this is the best location to see hares. Daisy and dandelion blooms are flowering. I scan the trees and nearby fields for fifteen minutes with no luck. Suddenly a pair, with their long rear legs, makes an appearance, running swiftly around in a madcap chase over open grassland. While they are not fighting or indulging in a boxing contest, they pause every so often to scrutinise the fields. Heads are turned abruptly, first one way, then the other, before they dart off at speed, true to the folkloric saying, 'As mad as a March hare'. In fact, this is not a sign of madness at all but an example of the courting behaviour of hares in the middle of their active breeding period. In *Season Songs*, Ted Hughes wrote of the hare in 'Deceptions': 'The March hare brings the spring / For you personally. / He is too drunk to deliver it. / He loses it on some hare-brained folly – / Now you will never recover it. / All year he will be fleeing and flattening his ears and fleeing – / Eluding your fury.'

From what I hear, and from the predictions of the grounds-man and woodmen, it promises to be a sunny summer. Posing on a branch, a beady-eyed collared dove scratches itself, launching into a series of nasal *cwurr-cwurr-cwurr* calls. It looks around circumspectly, then continues scratching. In 'The Shepherd's Calendar', published in 1827, John Clare wrote: 'March, month of many weathers wildly comes / In hail and snow and rain and threatning hums.' My wall calendar informs me that the date, 15 March, is the Ides of March (meaning the middle day of the month), best known as the day in 44 BC when Julius Caesar was assassinated. Caesar had been in political trouble, hence the soothsayer's warning in Shakespeare's immortal line: 'Beware the Ides of March.'

There is no dispute about the significance of the date two days later: 17 March, St Patrick's Day. I watch a crow and two bulky feral pigeons perform a clumsy jig, bordering on what could best be described as a wiggle dance, on a long, shaky sycamore branch. It may well be their way of celebrating the patron saint and there is a strong green iridescence to the pigeons' neck patches. The scene is crying out for rousing fiddlers, tin whistlers and box players to complement the mournful and prolonged pigeons' *proowoo-proowoo-proowoo*. Within a few minutes one of my musical wishes is fulfilled as starlings start their shrill whistling from a far-off tree.

After winter hibernation, each day brings something new,

accompanied by a noticeable warming of the sun. Insects are on the wing, and the place is alive with sound, movement and a restlessness, especially among birds moving purposefully in different directions, staking out territories, carrying twigs for nests, looking for mates and laying their eggs. Many are simply revelling in the sheer joy of the flight. A mob of house sparrows monopolises the bird feeders which we set out in early spring. Compared with other birds, sparrows are drab with a dull plumage and lack any natural singing ability. However, despite their 'Plain Jane' status, they have strong vocal cords, repeating their *chirp-chirp* every few seconds. Through binoculars I make out their black bib as they scan their surroundings inquisitively. One in particular loves the highest branch.

After the twists, turns, somersaults and unpredictability of the weather, flipping between cold and mild, the commotion of March has a gathering excitement that can best be absorbed by living close to nature. Occasional days are consumed with heavy rain, causing rivulets along the paths. Weather forecasters try to keep their options open through what is known as 'hedging', to make it sound better and to cover all eventualities. Their phrases and euphemisms include 'a mixed bag of sunshine and showers', 'wet and cold', 'unsettled few days', and the obvious-sounding 'It's cold out there' (raising the frightening prospect of what the weather indoors might be) or the apologetic 'It's not very spring-like weather, I'm afraid to say.' The worst cliché of all, though, is the anticipation of a storm with the inevitable precursor warning: 'Batten down the hatches.'

Depressions are coming in over Ireland, loaded with rain. Heavy downpours and grey skies are to be a feature of the week.

The torrential rain is non-stop and is accompanied by hail. I complain to my journal for the third consecutive day that it is coming down in relentless sheets, confining me to the cottage, since it is pouring at such a velocity that an umbrella is ineffectual. I am reminded of a Shakespearean quote from *Twelfth Night*, where the fool Feste closes the play with a song containing the refrain: 'The rain it raineth every day.' As I listen to the rhythm of the rain hammering on the cottage roof, I notice that the gutters and downpipe are under pressure. The singing kettle cheers me up and I jot down phrases used for the kind of rain in which Ireland specialises: bucketing, chucking, lashing, pelting, squally, pouring, a downpour, pissin' down. Skite of rain is a light drizzle, and mizzle is a marriage of mist and drizzle, spitters are small raindrops, while the term 'soft rain', which I have always thought of as an oxymoron, is still heard in places, along with 'soft day'.

An old March saying that may have credence states: 'When the days grow longer, the cold grows stronger.' But whoever said March is a watershed between winter and spring is correct, as the rain continues unabated in a stubborn fashion. At one point, I capitulate, and in the interests of assessing the power of the torrent, head out to face the worst. Biting hail showers sweep in horizontally, spattering my face, stinging my cheeks and flying into my mouth. The wind pushes tears from the corners of my eyes. Using gloved hands to shield my face, I dive behind a tree for refuge, which naturally makes matters worse. Hailstones the size of peas splatter through the branches with a vengeance, hitting the ground like thundering pellets; this used to be known in parts of Ireland as a 'cow-quaker', a phrase describing a rainstorm so heavy that cows shake.

The deluge, often referred to as 'wet rain', lasts for a few minutes before the mist closes in again but is quickly carried away by the force of the wind. Not so much a walk as a squelchy trudge, the day is exacerbated by the fact that a crack has emerged in my trainers allowing water to seep in. I retreat indoors, a drenched and bedraggled figure with chapped lips, soaked socks, trousers, shirt and jumper, dripping waterproof jacket that challenges the accuracy of the trade descriptions act, and an umbrella that is about as much use as a parachute in a submarine. Rain, some say, can nourish the soul, but the enjoyment gained from walking in it and embracing it is, to say the least, negligible, if not dispiriting. The hill walker Alfred Wainwright (nicknamed 'Rainwright') liked to say, 'There is no such thing as bad weather – only unsuitable clothing' – but that is a matter of opinion.

The downpour has a cleansing effect on the woods. When I venture out again, the upside is the sweet, earthy smell that envelops me, known as 'petrichor'. It comes from two ancient Greek words: *petros* meaning stone, and *ichor*, which refers to the fluid that flowed in the veins of the gods. The term was chosen to highlight the link between the earth and the air, which is fundamental to the release of the scent during heavy rain. The post-pluvial, or after-rain, effect also leads to activity by common snails, since the rain helps keep their skin moist. They are attracted to wet days, feeding on decaying vegetation, shrinking back into their shells in warmer weather, sealing themselves inside. Out-buildings and dustbins are their favoured territory. The rain has led to large oval-shaped pools of water lying in parts of the woodlands. Winnie-the-Pooh once declared, 'When life throws you a rainy day, play in the puddles.' Although some birds enjoy a puddle-fest, others deliberately avoid them. Bedraggled 'hoodies' high-step around them, like they're performing a group dance. While they are known for their ability to adapt to new environments, these birds are not happy on wet ground, looking for all the world in need of wellingtons.

When the rain finally relents in mid-afternoon, the woods come alive again with a musical magnetism. The time has arrived for unseen courtships, which will soon lead to mouths to feed. It is a perfect opportunity to see the birds as they emerge from undercover. A solitary male pot-bellied mistle thrush with heavy black spotting stands on the branch of a tall tree with an alert, upright stance, before taking off. I notice its eccentric flight, a slow rolling trajectory moving between trees, after which I have the good fortune to be treated to a virtuoso recital. Its repeated and continuous far-carrying fluting *prrr-rr-rr-rr* rattle is a sign that spring may not be far away. The mistle thrush is known for its superciliousness as much as for its gregarious nature. The male likes to have its distinctive voice heard, while the females are homemakers busily building their nests, collecting grass and earth for the high forks in trees. Owing to its habit of singing through the rain, it is called a 'Stormcock', while in Scotland the bird is given a folk name 'Big Mavis'.

Against a greying sky, four rowdy rooks, *Corvus frugilegus*, meaning 'fruit-gathering raven', are busy constructing stick nests high up in the canopy, expending considerable time on the task and using any material they can get their claws on. An ancient folklore saying states: 'Nests built in high tree branches mean a sun-filled summer, nests built in low branches a rainy summer.' Through binoculars, I watch them cawing in a shouty, boisterously agitated manner with their *kraa* call, which sounds like *aaar*. Rooks are renowned for stealing sticks from their neighbours' nests and there is a 'twig war' in progress, although it is hard to make out exactly what is happening so high up. When they come down to a field in a search for crops or fruit, I count a baker's dozen sitting on a fence, inky and sheeny, with an intense focus, before they lift off again, tumbling over tall trees in an even louder raucous cacophony. The collective noun for rooks is appropriately 'a building of', although they are also referred to as a congregation, a clamour and a pack.

Early spring is capricious. In the next few days longer stretches of daylight and glimmers of sunshine on tree blossom are an antidote to the foul weather. A magpie bullets past the cottage window clumsily carrying in its beak a stick about eighteen inches long. Wood pigeons, also called 'woodies', indulge in conspicuous display flights, announcing through their broadcasts that they own the territory below them. Along one of the back lanes that runs to the Low Wood, I spot two of them clambering among ivy bushes for ripe berries. Cock pheasants venture into the fields looking for beetles or ants. They fly up with loud squawks, their long tails fluttering, before dropping swiftly for cover behind the nearest bush.

At the very end of March, I anticipate a clear night. The air is frosty and lures me out to the lake, jacketed, hatted, scarved, gloved and booted for a bone-chilling night walk in the black velvet darkness, the major advantage being that there is no light pollution. The birds have gone to bed, but for other nocturnal animals it is a time of refuge. The night sky at first looks an impenetrable dark mass, though slowly my eyes adjust to the enormous sky, while underneath, on a slow meandering walk, I find a firm footing on dry tarmac. There is romance in the sight of a full midnight moon. It appears plumb and bright on the water of the serene lake, cloaking all it touches in a delicate silvery cloth.

The moon, now at its full-orbed peak and looking down on me, is known as a 'Worm Moon' because it coincides with the time when the earth begins its spring thaw and earthworms start to emerge from the soil.

I have long been intrigued by the fact that the English word 'lunacy' comes from the Latin *luna*. There is a belief, dating from ancient times – as the saying goes 'many moons ago' – of a connection between the moon and our mental state. The Greek philosopher Aristotle declared that a full moon brought with it a 'high tide' in certain people, in the form of frenzied behaviour and psychological instability.

I stare up at the moon, conscious of the first lines of William Henry Davies' poem 'Leisure': 'What is this life if, full of care, we have no time to stand and stare.' While the sky is pinpricked with a million or more creamy points, the Milky Way is visible as a faint smudge as my night vision kicks in. There may be an element of truth in the frenzied behaviour of animals rather than humans. The period from December to March represents the time of the fox mating season and the primal stillness of the night is disturbed by the shriek of a vixen coming into heat, an alarming blood-curdling cry piercing through the wooded darkness followed by a pause and then a bark. Although I am unable to see them, a fox's eyes contain a layer of reflective cells behind the retina, which shines light back into the eye, so that low light is significantly enhanced. Foxes also use the sensory whiskers on their faces and legs, which means they can make their way in the dark between obstacles by detecting airflow.

Some animals utilise moonlight as a vital navigational tool and being out in the witching hour brings a new sensory alertness. As I walk slowly along the circuit of the path from the front to the back gates, I listen to the soft flutter of bats' wings. When I plunge into the even deeper blackness of woodland, nocturnal noises abound. There is the soporific call of a long-eared owl, the soft two-second *hoo-hoo* vowels settling in the air over the lake. The paths and water glow in the ivory light. Tall trees around the edge of the path hiss with susurration, running through the gamut from a whisper to a drone. Birds have said their vespers and they are in their dreamtime sleep. The night not only offers rest but concealment and sanctuary. My eyes swivel around the forest, and paraphrasing Samuel Beckett, it is time to, 'Look again, look better', to see the pale ghosts of moths flickering in the stillness. In the tranquillity, I embrace the forest smell, recalling a line from Elizabeth Bishop's poem 'The Man-Moth' (a newspaper misprint for 'mammoth'): 'He does not see the moon; he observes only her vast properties.'

This is especially true at night when there is less distraction from the daylight sight and flight of moving creatures. My walk reveals unidentified chuckles and squeaks, part of the appeal of a wander through the darkness. I have read that almost 70 per cent of the world's animals are nocturnal, and for good reason. Creatures that feed by night exploit sources of food that are also taken by daytime animals, but without coming into competition.

The Montalto skies are a special part of our stay and clear nights are often decorated with stars. On another night-walk a heavenly light appears in the pitch-black sky, known as zodiacal light. In some parts of the United States, the Native Americans were 'lunar gardeners', while the Celts had a ritual of waiting until the fifth day of the new moon before picking mistletoe. There are beliefs that the moon may cause foliage in certain plants to lift and that moonlight influences seed germination, although it is not known why. In an essay 'Night and Moonlight', Henry David Thoreau brought his sharp eye to bear on the visual appearance of the night-time world: 'The leaves of the shrub-oak are shining as if a liquid were flowing over them … The woods are heavy and dark. Nature slumbers. You see the moonlight reflected from particular stumps in the recesses of the forest, as if she selected what to shine on.'

Sadly, one of Ireland's best-loved birds, the nightjar, no longer breeds here. This is a pity, as I have memorably heard their *chonk-chonk-chonk* on my travels in France, frequently just before dawn. As the gamekeeper told me, if you want a 'nightjar' the only place you will come across it locally is in the Century Bar.

A notorious reputation surrounds late March, which is known for its dreary, wet and windy weather, or if luck persists, some blinks of sunshine. The last three days of the month are referred to as 'borrowed days' from April. A Spanish folktale recounts how a shepherd promised to give March a lamb if the weather would stay calm for his flock. But when March delivered fine weather, the shepherd changed his side of the bargain and refused to give up the lamb. In revenge, March borrowed three stormy days from April and delivered raging winds to punish the shepherd.

***

Having been abroad for a week's holiday, we return refreshed to our cottage in mid-April and discover the estate looking like it has been given a spring-clean. The trees, in reality, are more suntanned than us. With revitalised energy and eyes, our senses perk up just as the sun is emerging to chase the clouds away and the gradual lengthening of light is perceptible. It helps to remind us of observing the changes in nature, exemplified in the Japanese word *Kisetsukan* – an awareness or sense of the seasons. My morning amble produces a stare-off with a young rabbit. Known as a kit, or sometimes called a 'kittie', it looks as if it has just left its nest as it munches slowly on leafy greens. Despite a nagging wind, moths skitter through the flowers browsing on the nectar. There are changes to the colour of leaves and the fronds of ferns are unfurling. Buds are swelling into life, while fresh shoots of bracken and seedlings vigorously push up to grab the sunlight; it is apparent that spring flowers have burst forth in considerable numbers.

On various dates towards the end of April and early May, a bird bonanza sweeps through the grounds to claim the spring and summer skies. African visitors, true to their own biological clock, arrive in the form of swallows, house martins and swifts. I focus on their aerial marvels and silhouettes darting around, trying to work out their identities. These fork-tailed birds return to the same colony each year with half of the pairs occupying the same nest. It is hard to pin down a definitive date for the arrival of the swifts from their prolonged migration journey in equatorial or southern Africa to Ireland. However, by the third week of April, their breakneck speed and accompanying screams are confirmation that they have safely arrived in Montalto. Reaching Ireland from their winter haunts requires a marathon perseverance, during which they overcome huge hazards, indulging in much-needed refuelling breaks in parts of Portugal or France, covering in some cases up to 515 miles per day. They value the grounds of the estate because there are old sheds and farm buildings where they set up home and they find the absence of human activity appealing.

High above the buildings, swifts torpedo through the sky on their curved-back wings, picking up aerial plankton. Known as 'Devil birds' because of their black plumage against the sky and haunting high-pitched screams, the swifts zip out of sight over the horizon of the roofs of outbuildings, suddenly reappearing. A considerable number, more than twenty, swirl around. Swifts intrigue me for their ability to stay in the air for a prolonged period and for the fact that they can sleep and navigate at the same time. Ornithology christens them *Apus apus*, derived from the ancient Greek *a* 'without' and *pous*, 'foot', based on the belief that the birds were a form of swallow that lacked feet. In the sky they look pitch-black, but the low sun turns their underwings bronze. They are blithely unaware, but in these solid stone buildings next to the cottage where they slip and dip out of the eaves, our worldly goods are stored securely in dozens of tea chests, cardboard boxes and packing cases. The rapidity of their movements and the speed at which swifts erupt around the woodlands is astonishing, as they chase, plummet and slice through the air.

Restless swallows have arrived too, flying five feet from the ground, skimming hedges, swooping in and out of farm buildings and carving their way around the grounds. They have come from southern Africa and crossed the Sahara Desert to reach Ireland, where they are renowned for their reliance on electric wires as a perch. Known under their old country name of 'barn swallows', they like a pastoral landscape, so the estate, with its empty buildings and the surrounding countryside, is perfect for them.

My antenna picks up clicking sounds reminiscent of a light being switched on and off. These calls are made by house martins, writing their calligraphy in the air after their spell in Africa and returning faithfully for spring and summer. With their blue-black and white plumage, and shallow forked tails, I admire their aerial displays, catching insects, wheeling and twisting in a frenzied activity. With its low solo run, a single house martin cuts in front of me, its pure white rump blazing.

There are half a dozen walks in the grounds where I regularly spend time. These routes, allied to a 'wander-where-you-will' approach, lead me to stumble across a variety of plants, shrubs and weeds. Near the entrance to the estate and in surrounding gardens, the pink cherry blossom has scattered its confetti-like petals on the ground. The annual regeneration of the woodland is a heart-warming sight bringing colour and vitality, and the season of procreation is underway with a sense of optimism. Shoots and tendrils are pushing through the soil and include dog roses and primroses. In Irish folklore, primroses were placed on the doorstep to encourage fairies to bless and protect the house and those who lived in it, and the demise of the flower offended the Sidhe or fairy folk. Bright yellow trumpets of daffodils crop up. They used to be referred to as 'daffadowndilly' and in Victorian times in Donegal their nickname was 'Tags'. When I see them, I am reminded of Ted Hughes' lines from 'Spring Nature Notes': 'A spurt of daffodils, stiff, quivering – / Plumes, blades, creases, Guardsmen / At attention / Like sentinels at the tomb of a great queen.'

Alongside daffodils, wood sorrel, with its pure white lilac-veined flowers above bright-green clover-shaped leaves, is producing its first flush. Vigorous nodding clumps of the delicate star-shaped wood anemones, which I christen 'wooden enemies', are certainly not enemies of a woodland, bringing agreeable tinges of pink, yellow and white to the floor. In romantic legends the wood anemone stars as a love flower, and ancient Greeks knew it as the 'wind-flower'. Daisies, or 'day's eyes', have taken over sections of the lawn sparkling in the sunshine, while another corner of greenery is the preserve of shiny yellow buttercups, traditional harbingers of spring, heralding warmer weather on the way. I find marsh marigold, also dubbed kingcups, and closer to the lake, the delicate, pale-pink lady's smock cuckoo flower, which likes damp meadows and grassy patches.

The floral domination comes through the appearance of large swathes of floppy bluebells scenting the air. The result is an immense smoky shimmer spread across parts of the woodland, hiding the ground with their intoxicatingly dark cobalt. In one heavily coated area, just off the main avenue, thousands of *Hyacinthoides non-scripta* (Latin for 'not written on') have taken over the undisturbed forest floor. It is difficult to make out where the flowers end, as they seem to vanish into the far distance in a hypnotic haze. A local name for bluebells in parts of Ireland is 'wild hyacinth', while in other parts of the country they are sometimes called 'blue rockets', and in Donegal 'crowpickers' or 'bummicks'. From long ago nature walks at school, I recall that in his novel *The Mayor of Casterbridge*, Thomas Hardy referred to the flowers as 'greggles'. With their floppy, elongated stems and thin load-bearing stalk, they are the most spectacular of flowers, since they face in a single direction. I crouch down and catch their sweet smell being released from the soft soil. The bluebell is also regarded as a flower of loss or an embodiment of sorrow. In *Fishing for Amber*, Ciaran Carson described them concisely: 'The bluebell, flower of mourning, tolls quietly in the dark woods.'

On a late April morning of *claritas* – Latin for clarity and brightness – the throb of mowers reverberating around the lake represents another quintessential sign of spring beginning in earnest, when the gardeners start cutting the large front lawn. As the energetic work gets underway, birds disappear because of the racket. The smell of freshly cut grass comes from a combination of chemicals and pheromones, known as green leaf volatiles. There is an obvious appeal to butterflies and bugs, which come out to inspect the work when it is completed, attracted by the musty smell of a pile of clippings, mixed with a lingering hint of ammonia and the pungent ingredient of petrol. Overall though, it appeals to my senses, as a freshness wafts on the air. The sight and smell of a lawn with symmetrical football-pitch-type stripes is linked to brighter and warmer days, with the optimism of more to come; I remain eternally grateful that I am not in charge of the extensive cutting operation.

The grass is appliquéd with buttercups, primroses and daisies, but in their wild abundance, humble dandelions steal the show. *Taraxacum officinale* – known as the living sun – are hardy plants that pop up everywhere and at odd angles in twos and threes. The French translation of the flower is the *dent de lion*, 'lion's tooth', a reference to the plant's tooth-like leaves. A few have a stumpy look, having fallen over as if resting, while those with a longer stem lean at angles. On closer inspection, I notice a mutation, with several two-headed dandelions compressed together, known as a fasciation or cresting. A bitter prejudice is held against dandelions by gardeners, who classify them as weeds and dislike their blooming on sprucely manicured lawns. They do not seem to bother those working here, but despite the scorn of the Montalto mowers they remain undimmed.

Those championing the downtrodden dandelion believe it should be the national flower of Ireland, a position long held by the shamrock, although it is not even a separate plant in its own right, but a corruption of an Irish word meaning 'little clover'. Few poets have extolled the flower's virtue, but in 'Spraying the Potatoes', Patrick Kavanagh refers to 'Dandelions growing on headlands, showing / Their unloved hearts to everyone.' As children we used to blow the fluffy flower's seed-heads, imagining we were telling the time. The number of puffs it took to remove all the seeds or disperse them in the wind was said to equal the hour of the day, which is why it was nicknamed the dandelion clock. In certain areas the dandelion is known as 'Jack-piss-the-bed', coming from the myth that even touching the plant will make you wet your bed. The flowers are most usually associated with dandelion wine. In France, I read that dandelions make a salad, *salade de pissenlits*, known for its diuretic properties.

***

The true hallmark of a bright spring is the dawn chorus – the morning concerto of bird music slicing through the air at the end of April, building to its peak at the start of May. From just after 4.30 a.m. the forest reverberates with a continuous rich, if jumbled, tapestry of sound. For many years I have been used to rising early to work shifts in a busy newsroom, starting at 6 a.m., but there has never been time to pause and listen to the long ribbon of birdsong. Instead, I had to endure the not-so-harmonious polyphony of loud and aggressive newsroom voices, the stale air thick with cigarette and pipe smoke accompanied by colourful language as we tried to find out about last night's incidents. Now, for nine consecutive days, the crooners of the air stir me from bed at the front of the cottage with their repeated pattern, an exuberant come-all-ye song saturation.

Collectively, they may have ruined my dreams, but the interruption is worth it. Seldom have I the chance to hear the symphonic purity of sound linked to romantic liaisons. The nature writer Mark Cocker states that the dawn chorus is not so much a united performance by the birds, but more 'their version of territorial warfare connected through music. The architecture of the sound,' he writes, 'doesn't even suggest the idea of a collective endeavour. It is more that period when each member of an orchestra plays randomly for themselves while tuning their instruments.'

My journal for the first morning – 30 April – records the time I awake as 4.37 a.m., with no need for an alarm clock. From then onwards there is little point in attempting to go back to sleep. The cacophony increases with a whistling, cawing and rich bubbling, and a certain amount of ad-libbing. A sudden burst of robin song is followed by the first bars of a blackbird and mistle thrush, before the rest of the forest stirs, with a deafening chatter in a pattern of lyrical randomness.

I indulge in an orange juice and energy bar and then, nursing a warming mug of coffee to sustain me, I quietly unlock the front door, stand outside by the window swaddled in a jumper and fleece, and train my binoculars on the songbirds. From the roof of the cottage the male blackbird belts out its baritone notes for several minutes with a 'here-I-am' bravado. If ever there was a conductor of a County Down birding choir, then the joyously unpredictable blackbird is the undisputed lead vocalist, although the thrush is not far behind in terms of a starring role. The mellifluously rich timbre and fruitiness of the blackbird's lazy chinking is an unmistakable rounded warble, with long pauses between the phrases.

Another blackbird sings with an endlessly inventive piercing but relaxed sweetness from a hawthorn twig and is so close that with every note I can clearly see the workings of its throat and trembling of its bright orange beak. In humans, the larynx, or voice box, sits high in the throat at the top of the windpipe, but the equivalent organ in birds is at the bottom of the windpipe and is known as the syrinx. In *The Charm of Birds* Sir Edward Grey says the song of the blackbird 'seems to make a direct appeal to us and stirs some inward emotion'. The joy of hearing and seeing the blackbird close up, pouring out its extraordinary song, is never to be forgotten. During the bright May mornings its deep, fluting aria and decibel level arouses my sensory system. Mark Cocker describes the blackbird's song as a 'fine, fresh distilled music of the temperate world – the very essence of the European spring'.

Along with the other songs, their cantatas resound through the woods, a complex and overlapping torrent of vocal dexterity of intense richness. More birds join in. The brassy fanfare-like sound of a plump song thrush pours out its intent, the energetic trill of the wren, and a burst of tits, all sounding as though they have been electronically amplified, along with the breezy two-note song of a chaffinch. Truly, my coffee cup over-floweth with gratifying euphonious bliss.

The liquid song of the robin lasts for up to fifteen minutes. It is believed they can utter a warbling sequence of a staggering 200 powerful phrases, the melodies rising out of nothing and sweeping through the whole gamut between hope and despair in a few seconds. Their quavering runs, and halted and fevered cascades, are often cut short by competing songs, which means that I lose count of phrasing and timing. W.H. Hudson's words – 'a musical confabulation' or 'corroboree' – play in my head.

All told, the dawn chorus is an uplifting soundtrack creating a reassuring sense of well-being and the feeling of a hospitable place. The singing and calling are a declaration of the arrival of spring and an unstoppable force of life echoing around the woods. But as well as an exhibition of bird happiness, it is an acceptance by them that they have survived a tough winter. There are many thoughts about the reason for the dawn chorus. The writer Lev Parikian believes that the term is misnamed, since 'chorus' is not the right word as it implies a togetherness and a unity of execution whereas the birds are intent on territorial rights. He states, 'We are the ones who attach further meaning to it, allowing it to infiltrate our hearts and lift our souls.' There is little doubt that this open-air theatre of song lifts our souls, and I remain in awe at how a large number of small throats can produce such a breathtaking audio panorama and complexity of musical notes.

Over the course of May, I note in my journal how the flora has bloomed to a prodigious verdancy in specific areas. Trees, leaves, hedges, grasses and a raft of plant life extend the colour scheme beyond the fabled forty shades. Around the lake, I come across a floral cornucopia including fieldwort, lady's fern and hart's tongue fern, woodwort, wood bindweed, cornmint and enchanter's nightshade. Tall reeds, lilies and yellow flag iris add to the plant mix. To one side of the lake and on another scale, gunnera, known as 'giant rhubarb', with its exotic umbrella-like leaves covered with bristly hairs, reflects in the water. It was introduced during Victorian times and is a familiar sight in many historic gardens, parks and botanical collections. Elsewhere, the overzealous tall canes of Japanese knotweed dominate, while greater willowherb, the strong-smelling three-cornered leek, ground elder, white sweet violet, water forget-me-not and stalks of woodrush all flourish. The botanical diversity burgeoning throughout the demesne is evidence of a late spring busyness.

A bouquet of pheasants darts across a laneway and a baby rabbit offers me a fleeting glimpse. The gamekeeper told me that for every rabbit I see there will up to twenty that I do not, even with beady-eyed vision. Against the drone of active insects in the background, butterflies are nettle-hopping, while bees hover around broom flowers before working their way in deep, then jumping to the next plant, fulfilling their pollination roles. Hundreds of winged insects are on the move: honeybees, wasps, hoverflies and numerous unidentifiable bugs all thrive by gathering pollen on what might be interpreted as a flower pub crawl.

***

Although I have walked and cycled all over the estate grounds, I have never properly explored the surrounding countryside. On a bicycle foray in late May around the lanes of The Spa on the periphery of the demesne, and along back roads, I pass through an archipelago of songbird territories with lusty singing. The sun is half in, half out and it is T-shirt weather. Bright yellowhammers are rasping from hawthorns, while others search for seeds. Their breeding season starts in late spring when they pair off and they nest on the ground in tall grasses near hedges or walls. Thrushes are chorusing louder than a ballad singer in the Century Bar, while meadow pipits, 'mipits' in birder's slang, chase one another in a weaving flight over the fields, their thin *tsip-tsip* ringing across farmland as they plunder hedgerows.

The wider landscape presents a tableau of the agricultural area. This part of mid-Down is a network of country roads and narrow lanes, generously endowed with hedgerows. John Deeres and Massey Fergusons dominate the roads and surrounding fields, farmed for corn and potatoes. Cattle are the mainstay but graffitied sheep protecting new-born lambs eye me with suspicion as I cycle around. The countryside is composed of swarms of drumlins or small hills rippling with pale green. The term 'drumlin' is derived from the Irish *droimnín*, meaning 'small ridge', referring to the shape of the hills formed under glaciers, and not to their composition. Drumlins are low, hog-backed mounds of soil, usually between fifty and ninety feet high, and in some cases up to a half-mile long. County Down has hundreds of them and they come with cattle, sheep, trees, fences, hedges and telegraph poles. In his definitive study *Mourne Country* (1951), which is in my cottage library, the geographer E. Estyn Evans describes drumlins as 'Little oval hills of drift, which are probably more numerous in the northern part of Ireland than in any other area of comparable size.' They give the countryside, he believed, a special character and a feeling of intimacy. 'They are normally disposed in fairly open order, with irregular patches of ill-drained bottom-land in between, from which they rise in bold sweeping curves.'

The road to The Spa is tunnelled with branches of overarching trees shading my route. In their late spring finery, they knit together in subtle browns, auburns and ochres, forming part of a multicoloured leaf canopy. The writer Paul Theroux describes such country roads with dappled light as having a 'sense of purification'. I leave my bike leaning against a sign and explore the roadsides. Long-established unkempt hedgerows foam with a tangle of bindweed, ragwort and the sharp spines of hawthorn. There are sprinklings of ash, oak, blackthorn and holly. I pause to absorb the heady scent of coconut and almond from the deep yellow gorse. Throughout Ireland, gorse is an archetypal part of hedge make-up and has a variety of names, including furze or whin; it is also used to flavour or add colour to whiskey. Gorse is associated with Lugh, the Celtic god of light, and with the spring equinox, although it flowers well beyond the first season of the year.

Hedges serve as more than just a fence representing the boundary between farms – they are also the borders where different habitats meet, providing ecologically rich environments. Just like the trees in the demesne, hundreds of plants and invertebrate species have been recorded in them. As well as providing flood defences and reducing soil erosion, hedges offer shelter, supporting birds and mammals, although few people, whether driving, cycling or walking, stop to admire their beauty. They are rich in fruits, salads and nuts that foragers have gathered for hundreds of years.

At ground level, I discover, the roadsides are edged with a riot of wildflowers, such as herb robert and the gold of dandelion. The sun now packs warmth and, as if to acknowledge the fact, bees emerge foraging for nectar. They delight in the pollen from the flowers and the honey they produce. The gold-spangled petals of lesser celandine with its dark-bronze leafage and short stems are a common sight in the verges. It grows in clumps but has passed its best and lost its gloss through dappled blotching. For flower-lovers it is known as the 'buttercup of spring', or 'spring's messenger', but I prefer its Irish nickname, 'brazen hussy'. English poets and writers such as D.H. Lawrence and Edward Thomas celebrated the flower, while Wordsworth had a special *grá* for it, espousing its cause and writing poetry to it: 'There is a Flower, the Lesser Celandine, / That shrinks, like many more, from cold and rain; /And, the first moment that the sun may shine, / Bright as the sun himself, 'tis out again!'

Umbels of the small, delicate white flowers of cow parsley, also called Queen Anne's Lace, froth the roadside margins of Montalto, while hoverflies show their fondness for the bounty of ragwort. I come across rosebay willowherb, bracken, dock leaves, tall nettles, ferns and the white foamy blobs of cuckoo spit, also known as froghoppers. Exuded by the spittlebug nymphs of sap-sucking insects, it has no connection to either frogs or cuckoos but is an important food source for swifts.

Around The Spa my ride takes me past a hubbub of neon vivid hedges, a wildlife corridor lined with dense constellations of bridal-white petals and yellow stamens of stitchwort, a bicycle showstopper. The flower is widespread along hedges, and clumps embroider the verges, a beacon of incandescence and contrast to the surrounding lush greenery. Also called 'stitch buttons', stitchwort is believed to have medicinal properties. It was apparently thus named because it was a childhood herbal cure for 'stitches', muscular cramps in the side.

Providing shelter and food, hedges are places of safety for wildlife but can also be the hidden location of tussles. I pull over to watch two small bright holly blue butterflies with black spots flirt around a tall hedge. They are hesitant in each other's close company, their contretemps lasting a few uncertain minutes, before they jink along the hedge in a figure of eight and disappear.

On my way back into the grounds a sign at a farm says, 'The bull charges, but the rest go free.' Two glossy blackbirds are enjoying a dose of vitamin D, lying on the front lawn with wings outspread, soaking up the rays. Our garden birdfeeder attracts blue tits jostling with a gift of robins for a share of the coconut bounty, an activity of to-ing and fro-ing that lasts for the afternoon. At times our nut hanger has become the preserve of the grey squirrels slithering up and down the pole.

On several spring mornings the tell-tale signs of what lawyers call 'circumstantial evidence' are visible and give me a jolt. Feathers strew the grass and I find scattered wings and small breast bones in various parts of the demesne, the hallmark of a kill known as 'bird carnage'. Although I am unable to make out which birds they came from, they are early morning ambushes with the remains of the grisly crime scenes still apparent. I look up across the sky but see only the distant contrails of an aircraft. The gamekeeper explains that occasionally a male sparrowhawk may attack any bird up to the size of a blackbird, or even as big as a mistle thrush, on which it would feed for a couple of days. They usually eat small mammals, but during the breeding season the sparrowhawk must provide food for his offspring, while the female birds may also make up to ten kills per day. This, he shrugs, is part of the natural order. Life goes on, a balance has to be achieved, and the predators have to live as well. Putting out a bird table, he says is like setting out a restaurant table for the bigger birds.

I reflect on the wonderment of nature, which reminds me of an example of the messy wildness of birding warfare; it is a difficult and dangerous life for small birds and can turn horribly cruel. Births and deaths happen all the time in the woods, often unseen. Sparrowhawks have even been known to catch bats. The writer J.A. Baker points out that the word 'predator' is baggy with misuse: 'All birds eat living flesh at some time in their lives. Consider the cold-eyed thrush, that springy carnivore of lawns, worm stabber, basher to death of snails. We should not sentimentalise his song and forget the killing that sustains.'

Summer

'It is interesting to contemplate a tangled bank, clothed with many plants of many kinds, with birds singing on the bushes, with various insects flitting about, and with worms crawling through the damp earth, and to reflect that these elaborately constructed forms, so different from each other, and dependent upon each other in so complex a manner, have all been produced by laws acting around us.'

Charles Darwin, *On the Origin of Species*

'The trees encountered on a country stroll
Reveal a lot about that country's soul.'

W.H. Auden, 'Bucolics II. Woods'

The sky is a bowl of pastel blue, summer has deigned to arrive and the cycle of life is reaching its annual peak. Nature does not fix an exact date for the end of spring and the arrival of summer, but crossing the seasonal threshold shows up aspects of the grounds in a different light. From a distance, the crowns of trees, such as beech and oak, appear to be on a collision course, or at least have interlinked in partnership making it difficult to see where certain ones start and end. However, when I stand under them and look up, surprisingly, I make out a thin line of sky separating them, so it is clear that they are not colliding. This is referred to by arboreal experts as 'crown shyness', where trees of the same species, and even those of different species, desist from getting up close and personal, refraining from touching each other by keeping a respectable distance. Opaque June beeches, Douglas fir (named after a Scottish botanist, David Douglas, born in 1799) and tall, thin birches are muffled by heavy branches laden with foliage. They are, to rephrase Yeats, in their summer beauty, with June breaking out all over. It is a time of lushness, a moment to savour.

For nine months I have been observing birds, many of them passerines. During that time I have ducked under the low-hanging branches of the sycamore, sometimes referred to as 'the hanging tree' because its lower limbs make suitable gibbets. But I also swung on bigger trees, climbing those strong enough to support my weight, and in a stepladder-to-the-sky activity reminiscent of childhood, grazing my knees. While I often thought about the trees, their history and the remarkable lives they lead, I never properly considered the branches that remain inconspicuous, playing second fiddle to the trunk and the grandiose aspects of a huge hazel or oak. On a languid afternoon walk through a mixed woodland of willow and ash, I discover a branch-communing paradise and try to separate boughs from the smaller twigs. They come in many shapes, sizes and forms – vertical and diagonal –

and are known under the Latin words *ramus* or *cladus*. Smaller branches are called branchlets, while the larger branches are known as under-branches, which look crooked and chaotic.

On a tall beech, I follow the pattern of an elongated branch reaching out into the avenue. At more than fifteen feet long it has a wavy shape and is pockmarked with lumps, bumps and dark knotty protuberances. In several places, birds have dropped their splotched messages of love. Two V-shaped branches spring from it halfway along, while at its end, the branch curls upward with a mix of crumbling leaves and full-flowered ones. I ponder over how certain trees survive longer than others, and wonder if there is a special secret related to soil, climate, age or time determining their height, how long they live and why some are happier in the shade than others. It is curious to discover that the height and position of branches fluctuate, and only rarely do they knock against one another. Quite a few are drooping; some are bare and thicker near the trunk, twisting and tapering out at the extremes or shooting upwards with five or six thinner tendrils smothered with leaves. I am conscious of what is known as Sudden Branch Drop Syndrome, which is self-explanatory. This can be triggered by bacterial wet wood or a surplus of moisture that weakens the tree's structure, but curiously is more common during hot, dry summer weather than in stormy conditions. Trees have been known to 'auto-amputate' by letting go of a limp limb.

My notes record the patterns on branches of some of the arrow-straight mature trees. On several of them, leaves are cascading like Rapunzel's hair, while others display the remnants of white buds long past their sell-by date. Strolling under trees and examining their branches is pleasurable. I sit up against

A variable group of carpet or ground-cover roses. (© Trevor Ferris)

Moody overarching branches of laurel trees at Ednavady hill lead to the
History Trail, focusing on where the 1798 rebellion took place.
(© Trevor Ferris)

Paul Clements at the reinstated wooden bridge in the rejuvenated Lost Garden uncovered in 2018. (© Trevor Ferris)

The blue mophead hydrangea is one of the plants providing late summer colour around the gardens. (© Trevor Ferris)

Right: The Low Wood has been transformed with the planting of thousands of new trees, while other parts of it continue to spread in a carnival of greenery.

Below: Tree trunks in parts of the dark Low Wood are furred with a glowing velvet moss due to their proximity to the Ballynahinch River, which affects humidity and temperature.
(© Trevor Ferris)

The Ballynahinch River flows through the edge of the estate from Dromore Street, joining with several other rivers before emptying into Strangford Lough. Dippers and kingfishers have been noted along the river. (© Trevor Ferris)

Japanese maple are among the most exotic trees found in the estate, leafing out in brilliant autumn reds. (© Trevor Ferris)

the bark of a maple tree reading a book of Billy Collins' poetry, specifically his 'Walking Under the Trees': 'I'm walking under the trees / walking in and out of their shadows / walking step by step under the trees / so the leaves on their lowest branches / graze my bare head / as I walk slowly under the trees / so close to me they could have / their arms around my shoulders, / walking under the guardian trees.'

The change to summer marks a transition, bringing shafts of sunlight catching dancing motes of dust. Sunbeams play on the paths and the woods are abuzz and abustle with a shifting profusion of insect life. The dense gallery of voluptuous green makes it difficult to see birds, but fragmented, stop-start chanting is intersected with short-lived, off-key bursts of song and excited cackles. A tiny fly, smaller than a fingernail, lands on my trouser leg, running up and down, developing a curious interest in the intricacies of my laces. It is in no hurry to depart. Obscured birds are not flaunting themselves in the same style as they were a month earlier. A blackbird sails across in front of me into the woods, then doubles back, alighting on the path and scouring his surroundings. He proceeds with a mix of hopping, shuffling and mini-runs, indulging in ground-feeding, his beak poking and turning over the soil searching for worms, insects or snails. A garbled blackcap melody comes from a far corner of the forest depths, followed by the urgent two-syllable *pitch-ew, pitch-ew, pitch-ew* whistle of a coal tit piercing the air.

Early morning sunshine drenches the estate in a golden light, bringing out the best in the lepidopterist world, one of the incontrovertible signs of summer. Tipsy butterflies, as if drawn by a magnet to flowers and bushes, launch aerial displays, fluttering about between yellow daisies or basking briefly on thistles. Over the course of an uncharacteristically hot period in June and a run of dry days, a hatch of enchanting butterflies speaks of early summer. On 24 June, as if in recognition of the feast day of St John the Baptist – a date closely associated with midsummer festivities – small tortoiseshells, meadow browns and red admirals traffic between a variety of flowers and bramble bushes – perhaps commemorating the occasion by holding their own feast day. The deep chocolate brown of the speckled wood, with cream markings on its forewings and hindwings, is a distinguishing presence which I bump into along a track. It has a particular fascination for feeding on fruits and bramble bushes. A cloud of holly blues, with sky-blue upper wings bordered in black, circles me cautiously; they are lured off their navigational course, then divert to shrubbery but are unable to settle for any length of time. Two common blues stagger around a hedge, fidgeting and sparring at high speed, which soon turns hesitant and uncertain. Briefly they link together, secretively getting up to tricks.

The fastest butterfly of all is the glamorous but petite male orange-tip, furiously intent on his business and with an eye for the ladies. His mind is not just on lady's-smock but is clearly filled with drink, from the nectar of flowers, and sex. With delightful orange pigmentation on the wings, I spot this species several times on hedges around the woodland edge, although their trajectory makes them difficult to see clearly. While the orange-tip's scientific name is *Anthocharis cardamines*, its popular nickname is 'the lady of the woods'. The name has more than one use in the woodlands, since the silver birch, one of the first trees to break into leaf, is known by the same epithet.

Childhood days are linked to butterflies, captivating encounters of exhibitionists from another world. Their glossy wings are reminders of long-ago hot summer days with two months off school to do as we pleased; a cycle ride through a sequestered valley, a wander over fields filled with earwigs, beetles and blowflies scavenging on cow dung, or a ride on top of a trailer loaded with hay were some of the supreme pleasures, linked to the recollection of seeing a red admiral, nicknamed by farmers as a 'red admirable'. In 'Fireflies', the Bengali poet Rabindranath Tagore wrote: 'The butterfly counts not months but moments. / And has time enough.'

The fat glitters of buff-tailed bumblebees are on their eternal quest for pollen and nectar. There is a superstition, or *piseog*, in Ireland that if a bumblebee buzzes at the window of a house, it is a sign of a coming visitor. Folklore also believes that the bees take offence easily, which leads them to no longer produce honey, deserting their hives and dying.

As I change my perspective, I regard the skill of other small masters of the air that are hanging with a stillness. A humbler and less flirtatious insect, the ladybird, characterised by its spots, likes warm weather. This tiny, seven-spotted beetle enjoys the slow munching of larval aphids on rose bushes and honeysuckle. Few insects have commanded such an array of sobriquets over the centuries in Ireland and Britain, where they are also known as ladybugs. Among the myriad names are goldie-birds, red-coats, ply-goldings, sodgers, clock-leddys, king alisons and little short red cow. In parts of England they were originally called 'Our Lady's Bird'. The first section of the name refers to the fact that during the Middle Ages the most common images of the Virgin

Mary showed her in a red dress. Their Latin name, *Coccinella septempunctata*, was associated with the Seven Joys and Seven Sorrows of Mary.

A stroll over the grass throws up moths flying at my feet in their subfusc colours. I have seen several of them on the curtains in our cottage, but they are hard to identify since there are 2,500 species, which is why they are mostly classified as moths or micromoths, the latter having a smaller wingspan.

Dozens, if not hundreds of tiny oval-shaped clover mites, known to science as arachnids or eight-legged arthropods – and familiar to gardeners as pests – zigzag their way around the grounds. They like hard surfaces such as bin lids or window ledges, but also lush plants, where they feast on dandelions and clovers. Most are an intense red, while others are reddish-brown. I try to trace their route, but they move at speed, chasing each other, then stop-starting as though confused, changing direction and racing onwards.

Shy insects, or at least those that are hard to see, dwell on the periphery of my attention. On an early morning stroll, and on another scale, two dragonflies flicker their wings, skittering across the lake, while curious-looking newcomers in the form of tiny hawk moths, a day-flying species, dry their wings on bushes. Close to the front of the big house they stick out their long tongues, hovering in mid-air before alighting on the arching shrubs of honeysuckle blossom. With their jewel-like appearance, damselflies are also on the move as dimples break out on the lake surface bestowing a welcome. As the Roman author, naturalist and philosopher Pliny the Elder noted: 'Nature is nowhere as great as in its smallest creatures.'

After another cut of grass, a plump party of ten feral pigeons invades the newly mown lawn, descending with a powerful whoosh. They seize my attention, grey on grey. Heads bobbing, they nibble quietly, moving purposefully, picking at seeds, plant material and invertebrates. With a steady uninterrupted flow and occasional pauses, they shuffle around, keeping a circumspect lookout for predators. Through binoculars, I focus on their conspicuous white neck patches, along with their grey-green head and purple gloss to the side of their neck. They exude serenity but also value their personal space as they spread themselves around, observing the principle of individual pecking distance. One of their flock wanders over to a bush while the others, like privates on parade, march slowly in single file across the length of the lawn.

Two more big-boned pigeons then arrive on another part of the grass, initially gliding down quietly, then launching into a jaunty dance which unexpectedly turns into a tumultuous and nasty mixed commotion of fluttering, flapping and flailing lasting several minutes. Is this, I wonder, an example of the spiritual power of *anam cara*, soulmates having a friendly row, a territorial battle, or a bizarre courting ritual of summer love? Their zigzagging tussles are gate-crashed by the arrival of crows disturbing the pigeons' animated duologue, which reaches a finale as they lift up obstreperously, orbiting in a dozen different directions. The crows may even have come to referee, although their discourse is cawing rather than whistling. They are clever birds who can count to four and recognise human faces – giving a lie to the phrase 'bird-brained', which ornithologists believe should be regarded as a compliment rather than a derogatory term.

From the leaf litter of forests and other habitats, snails and slugs are a feature of life. Although generally more active under cover of darkness or in heavy rain, I find them in stone cracks, under flowerpots, between path slabs, beside the bins and inside the lids. Garden snails are more common, gliding across the grass, but are disliked by gardeners because they thrive in causing damage, eating holes in leaves, stems and flowers. According to the groundsman it is hard to eradicate them as there are few preventive measures. But the molluscs like to indulge in a degree of selectivity, since there are some herbaceous plants to which they are less likely to be drawn. In parts of Ireland, they feature in folk medicine for curing warts. The warts are rubbed with a snail, which is then impaled on a tree, and as the snail dries up it withers away while the warts also disappear. The visible slime trail produced by snails has been used in many cultures for treating a variety of minor wounds and skin ailments, such as psoriasis or eczema. Around the manicured lawn and lake's edges, skunk cabbage, with its yellow and white flowers, is prevalent during June, while the blue flowering slender speedwell and daisies adorn the grass.

***

'The clearest way into the Universe is through a forest wilderness', wrote the environmentalist and backwoodsman John Muir. And there is no question of the mysterious allure attached to the numinous, otherworldly and little-visited old forest known as the Low Wood. The demesne boasts several mixed groves, which include the Low Wood, located beyond the lake and extending to the Ballynahinch River and Dromore Street. It has been allowed to run wild and for me it is a hitherto unexplored corner of the estate: 'The woodland that time forgot', as it is called. This damp, gloomy and darkly atmospheric, jungle-like place comes with a canopy of venerable, tall trees with fan vaulting. Even on a July day little sunlight filters through, and it is a mystical grove with a sense of *uaigneas*, an Irish word meaning eeriness, loneliness, longing or a feeling of sadness being away from people.

A pallid place, the Low Wood has a primeval feel, steeped in its own rhythm of action and pin-drop silence, glowing with a verdant luminosity. It is an enormous wood of 40,000 acres, where the arboreal variety ranges from cathedral-height down to bulging trees – known as 'old knobblies' – their stumps strangled with dead or rotting bracken. Gnarled species with contorted limbs and humongous girths are locked in embrace, twisted branches intertwining and looking like feuding neighbours. Others have hollow trunks and one oak has taken on a Buddha-like shape, while close by stumps of trees are covered in a proliferation of ivy. A few scrawny examples stand to one side, their future uncertain. The Latin name for moribund trees, decaying wood and fallen sticks, coupled with an all-encompassing ecology of fungi and microbes, is *saproxylic*. As well as fungi featuring the caps and stalks of mushrooms, the non-flowering plants here are less glamorous and include ferns, mosses, liverworts and lichens.

The wood is an intricate network of neglected beech, alder, birch, oak, sycamore, laurel and willow, and has been allowed to run amok. Some trees are split into two stems, broken, bent or under stress with fungal disease. Near the Ballynahinch River, the trunk of a single towering beech is furred with a blancmange of glowing velvet moss around its entire girth, caused by the damp climate coming off the river. For its part, the river twists and turns for more than one mile through the edge of the estate. Montalto marks the beginning of its life, before it flows into the Annacloy River, then morphs into the much bigger Quoile River running through Downpatrick before emptying into Strangford Lough. Curiously, the trunks of certain trees deeper in the wood are only half covered with moss since the dampness does not affect them to the same degree.

Shrubs and ragged flowers, alongside an array of fiendishly long and opportunistic thistles, thorns and briers entwine with blackberries and a profusion of willow. On this summer afternoon, I stumble across an area that nature has overwhelmed with chest-high nettles, sprawling clumps of brambles, dock, hogweed and hunks of standing wood. Few footprints have walked this way for many decades and there is an enigmatic mystery with a muted and musty sensation. It is often said that a centuries-old wood calms the mind, eases stress and is an enchantment to the personality of its revelatory silence. It is a secret place where I unlock my mild dendrophilia fetish. I am not a dendrologist, nor have I ever 'graduated' to tree-hugging status – just some gentle bark-stroking or branch-caressing. However, I conclude that the best way to get closer to nature is to remove my socks and trainers, tiptoeing gingerly through the wood to further my study of the barks. As I wander barefoot and feel the grass underfoot, it brings a new concentration on the quiet muttering of the forest. Looking carefully at where I am stepping brings an awareness of the crunch of beech mast, the plush ground-hugging moss, and the texture of fallen leaf mould, bare wood and flaking bark. In 1945 the Scottish writer Nan Shepherd suggested that 'walking barefoot has gone out of fashion, but sensible people are reviving the habit'. Many now believe that it brings positive health benefits, affecting mood and well-being.

Jackdaws add to the moodiness, and I feel like a trespasser, stumbling on the fabric of a strange hidden world of deformed trees with burrs and swellings, the inosculation of root buttresses and barks fusing together with conjoined branches. No wonder Oliver Rackham, the tree maestro, described them as 'mysterious beings that we can never fully understand'. There are few paths to follow, but with the dappled shade it is a place of sanctuary – until a magpie startles me by crashing out of a bent tree. The alarm calls of other birds ring out from oaks, bulbous old giants with troll faces and knotted branches still sprouting leaves, a testament to their longevity. In some cases, the bark has a distinctly corrugated surface, while the texture of others is coarse. They show a mix of fissures and criss-cross patterns, a few are flaky, patchy and come with outgrowths. In another corner the barks are puckered with cracks, while some are smooth and papery.

As a fine summer drizzle begins, accompanied by a breeze, I emerge from under a huge, twisted beech tree, its trunk green with algae and trembling branches, and its flayed roots bearing an uncanny resemblance to the shape of an elephant's foot. In another area, dead leaves, sticks and twigs are clustered at the base of an oak tree in what is known as 'wind flotsam', where the roots have formed a type of net catching anything passing on the wind. Each species of tree has its own texture of bark, many with remarkable colours and unusual shapes. A world of greenery envelops me. I note the mushy green of peas, mint green, the green of washing-up liquid, but the wood is also interwoven with a patchwork of other colours. These feature the shining red berries of lords and ladies scattered across the woodland floor, alongside a floral repertoire of botanic richness of pignut, dog violet, yellow pimpernel, chickweed and speedwell. Barks are amber, chocolate brown and grey, while others range from bright lime green to dark emerald. The surroundings bring an understanding of the variety of green found in both plants and minerals. On the palette of the painters' chart, 'Forest stroll' may represent some aspects of the Low Wood, but 'Tropical jungle' better epitomises the scale of colours, since there is a lush feel to it.

Beneath my bare feet and under the faded leaves of wood sorrel lies an intricate network of mycorrhiza fungal threads linking plants to the soil, which help the trees communicate with each other. There are reminders here of storms and of bulging trunks blown down. The ground is a soggy mat of leaves, grass and twigs, and when I step on a stick, it cracks like a gunshot. Unfazed by my presence a blackbird enters the stage. Its position remains unchanged for five full minutes and a stillness reigns. Across the soil, worms move at their own deliberate pace as I reflect on the fact that Darwin once said that he doubted any other animal had 'played so important a part in the history of the world'.

The variety of plants provides a host of microhabitats used by tiny insects and invertebrates, which in turn are a food source for birds. In the short turf, tiny funnel webs of spiders look delicate, while a wren alights searching for morsels. The pulse of insect life is a secretive world, but noises play out in the undergrowth. I come across water beetles, jumping spiders and hoverflies, which are marvels of flight hanging in the air, holding their position as if pinned to it. A clicking sound from another area attracts my attention. The tiny click beetle with its narrow thin legs is a curious little creature, which has an inbuilt spring. I watch in awe as it turns itself over on leaves, falls to the ground sniffing decaying roots, then jumps into the air before slipping off into the undergrowth.

The dead wood has its uses. A two-banded longhorn beetle, so-called because of two prominent yellow bars on its wings, appears on a rotting conifer, preparing to bore in deep to lay its eggs in the dead bole. The larvae live in dead wood and take several years to mature. The American wildlife writer Peter Matthiessen often focused with a minute mindfulness on what he called 'the great pleasure in the awareness of small things'. For him this could be a tree, a flower, a beetle, a frog or grasshopper or even a click beetle.

I change my own focus from the ground to the tops of the trees, since I have often been puzzled about forest canopies. They are the unfathomed realms of nature because, unless you are an arboreal expert with an extension ladder, a crane or a hot air balloon at your disposal to gain access, then you will never know with certainty what goes on in the higher reaches of forest life. Aloft in the air, exploring this unknown world featuring the crowns of trees would be a special treat. The dark-green depth of canopy knowledge is confined to sparrowhawks and kestrels, competing in higher air space.

The Low Wood is a sanctuary, an ethereal place of hushed sounds, somewhere to still the mind and empty the body of anxiety, and it has evolved into my *locus amoenus*. More than three hours of tree-gazing has drifted past, and I come out onto a path, pulling on my socks and shoes, feeling that I have identified with the energy and spirit of an old woodland. As I leave, there is the feeling of a light being turned on and two birds dart past so fast that I cannot make them out. I call to mind the poem 'Trees' by Ted Hughes: 'Trees, it is your own strangeness, in the dank wood, / Makes me so horrifying / I dare not hear my own footfall.'

Montalto is a rich place to reconnect with nature but also to reflect on the tapestry of past lives that we know little about, apart from old photographs or archival documents. We can measure the span of our short lives against trees, and the woods evoke time and a constantly changing landscape. In my mind's eye, I have thought about the people who previously came to enjoy the grounds, walking through the gardens when they were open to the nattily dressed local drapers, the clergy and the public. The men sported beards and braces, while the women, who brought the picnics, wore long elegant dresses, shawls, hats or bonnets and carried parasols. Young children in knickerbockers excitedly played games, revelling in the experience.

***

By mid-July lingering flowers include the appropriately named ragged robin and colonies of nodding harebells. In mythology, harebells belonged to the fairies, who would cast a spell on anyone trespassing through them. The name comes from the superstition that hares were the companions of witches. Rabbits, squirrels and frogs are all part of the sociable silvicolous world. The leafy crowns of the mature oak, beech and lime trees form an unbroken layer across the canopy of the forest. Little, if any, sunlight is able to penetrate through to the carpet floor.

The woods are falling quiet and the birds are calling a halt to their singing as the GJS – the Great July Silence – sweeps across the estate, a period that is also known as the 'midsummer silence'. It is so quiet that for the first time the sound of traffic on the roads skirting the grounds is audible, along with barking dogs. On a walk near the golf course, I pin back my ears when I overhear that someone has 'scored a birdie'. This term is, of course, nothing to do with the creatures of the air, since it represents a score of one stroke under par. It comes from the American slang term 'bird', meaning anything excellent, and has a considerably different connotation from viewing winged airborne flyers.

Towards the end of the month, in 'high summer', songs can still be heard, but most birds indulge in hushed or low-murmur conversations that are not urgent. This period represents the last hurrah of claiming territorial rights along with the occasional high-pitched cry of nestlings. Others, such as pigeons and robins, are shedding their feathers, which have suffered wear and tear, over-exposure to ultraviolet light, or general deterioration. As their feathers start to moult to their autumn or winter plumage, it is as if they are changing into a new outfit. At this stage of their lives, they are more vulnerable than usual, which is why they remain quiet, preferring to stay out of sight. Rooks and jackdaws are also in moulting mode, waiting for their new flight feathers, and are drained of energy, appearing occasionally with a gaunt look. I do, though, see a couple of mischievous magpies wander across the lawn, while a mini-parliament of hooded crows plays a half-hearted hop-a-long game on a path. The American poet Helen Hunt Jackson summed up the quietude of this time of year: 'Silence again. The glorious symphony / Hath need of pause and interval of peace. / Some subtle signal bids all sweet sounds cease, / Save hum of insects' aimless industry.'

A sudden rumble of thunder breaks the tranquillity, with three successive deep peals. Within a minute the sky turns dark, while quick flashes of lightning-strikes scare the squirrels and a deluge is underway. Nature is going through a purple patch as we approach our final month in the cottage. More scattered showers skipping through the woods are followed by shafts of light, before a dazzling rainbow makes an appearance in a huge arc across the sky, turning into a double bow.

Early in August my journal records the peculiar appearance of fresh summer buds on younger rather than mature plants or trees. A cycle along the tracks reveals a wave of new shoots and leaves – a so-called 'second coming' – most vigorous in oak, ash and sycamore, as well as conifers. I park my bike to inspect this remarkable regrowth, which is apparent at the tips of branches where dappled lime-green leaves have sprouted in contrariety to the older and darker green leaves. At their extremities, trees and shrubs are flecked with tints of pale yellow, light pink, violet and pastel blue. The brightest are oak trees, where leaves turn into a semi-glossy red. The colours are mostly visible to my naked eye and are another pointer of the vibrancy of the seasons moving through the woods, even though the main growth rush is over.

This strange but refreshing phenomenon of a new surge of energy in branches is known as 'Lammas growth', or 'Lammas leaves', since it occurs around 1 August, Lammas day, halfway between the summer solstice and the autumn equinox. Originally a Celtic feast celebrating the sun god Lugh, it is now known as Lúnasa. In the Christian calendar Lammas, which derives its name from 'loaf-mass' or 'loaf festival', celebrates the earliest fruits of harvest, when bread made from the year's first ripe corn was taken into church as an offering, marking the start of harvest. The period is chiefly observed in north Antrim, where two days of dancing, horse-trading, bargaining, street markets and traditional music take over the streets of the coastal town of Ballycastle for the Ould Lammas Fair during the last Monday and Tuesday of August. Even though the shoots persist for a few days, they are a surprise, since I often thought of August as a stale and muggy month, reflecting the suffocating days of high summer, and an ideal time to escape for a day out to the hills.

For eleven months Slieve Croob, ten miles south-west of Montalto, has been beckoning me seductively, and with the long evenings I opt for a change of scene. A walk to the top of Croob stretches my imagination as well as the hamstrings, as I digress from the woods to breathe in mountain views. The drive on country roads through Dromara passes roadside hedges of bindweed and ragwort, competing with ox-eye daisies and cow parsley, alongside stands of purple loosestrife. From Dromara, I head to Finnis and turn on to Dree Road, a long, hilly and narrow track with passing places and more tractors than cars. It is a forty-five-minute walk to the top of Croob under a sky of gleaming blue. Tall clumps of grasses and plants, such as the waist-high spear thistles with their bouquet of fluffy purple seed heads, line both sides of the uphill route.

Even though they are wizened, the thistles are beloved of finches. In this case, gangs of greedy greenfinches precede me on the path, thistle-hopping as they bounce along up to twenty feet ahead in what amounts to a mini-bombardment. Trying to count them is impossible, and because of their endearing butterfly display flight, they appear and disappear with rapidity, although I estimate that collectively there are at least forty in the different parties. Their striking yellow wings stand out in the sunshine along with their olive-green hue and tail-flapping, while another giveaway is their repetitive liquid *chit-chit-chit*. Farther along, fat and furry bumblebees buzz around my hat and rucksack before disappearing in search of nectar to boost their energy levels.

Slieve Croob, which is the source of the River Lagan, is an outlier of the Mourne Mountains and holds a historic place in the lives of local people. The hill and its surrounding moorland played a significant part in the 1798 uprising, since it was in this area that many of the United Irish rebels hid. It is 1,752 feet high, and the summit stones were piled into small cairns, now known as the 'Twelve Cairns', named after the remains of a prehistoric burial cairn on its pinnacle. Its name in Irish, *Sliabh Crúibe*, means 'the mountain of the hoof'. This is sheep country par excellence, where hundreds of woollybacks rest peacefully in the folds of hills or in quiet pockets. Holly, bramble, blackthorn and whins survive among the boulders where they escape the attention of sheep. On the lower slopes, heather has colonised rocks, but at the top vast swathes of it dominate in a multi-coloured mosaic ranging from a fiery red, bordering on tints of magenta, to an orangey-yellow.

Alongside the natural sound of greenfinches and skylarks, there is a 360-degree view from a trig point close to a transmitter station and radio mast. One hundred years ago, in the 1890s, the botanist, writer and polymathic figure Robert Lloyd Praeger described Slieve Croob as 'wild and bare, and one's chief reward in climbing it, apart from a bracing and health-giving walk, is the grand view which is obtained from its summit'. Lying to the north, I make out the rounded tops and blanket bog of the Sperrin Mountains, shared between Tyrone and Derry, with the large expanse of Lough Neagh to the east. Both Divis and Black Mountain near Belfast stand out, as well as Belfast Lough, Scrabo Tower and Strangford Lough.

The near-distance consists of smaller sister peaks forming the rugged foothills of the Dromara hills. It is a landscape of compact lakes and streams, drumlins and farmland. Scatterings of houses and cottages are dissected by hedges, forest parks and plantations, intersected with hamlets and towns. Fields have been ploughed, the soil loosened and weeds uprooted, while combine harvesters are working overtime. Lyrical townlands echo in the placenames, a reminder that nature belongs everywhere. Drumnasade: 'Bridge of the Needle'; Drumaness: 'Bridge of the Waterfall'; Creevy-tenant: 'Tree of the Assembly'; Ballycreen: 'Townland of the Withered Wood'; Ballymaglave: 'McGlave's Holding'; Maghera-knock: 'The Green Ridge'; Magheratimpany: 'McAtamney's Plain'; Magheradrool: 'Plain Between Stream Forks'; Ballylone: 'Townland of the Fattened Lamb'.

For a change of view, I focus my binoculars on the high Mourne Mountains, a distant *tableau vivant* to the south beyond Castlewellan. Crammed in hugger-mugger fashion, the classic sweeping view of the Mournes reveals their shapely prospect and is a reminder of our smallness. With a purity of outline on this clear summer evening, they are an enchanting presence. As a toponymist, it is a pleasure to recite mountain names and, west to east, they trip off my tongue with easy familiarity: Donard, Commedagh, Bearnagh, Meelmore and Meelbeg, and south to

Doan and the Binnians. The alluring placenames of 'the Kingdom of Mourne', such as Hare's Gap, Brandy Pad, Bloody Bridge and Devil's Coach Road, come with historic tales, their paths linked by the Mourne Wall.

Building work on the wall – overseen by the Belfast Water Commissioners – started in 1904 but was not completed until 1922. The workers made their own chisels, cut and dressed the stone on site, and referred to the wall, which snakes its way up and over the mountains for twenty-two miles, as the 'Back ditch of Mourne'. But in his Thomas Davis Lecture on Radio Éireann in December 1956, E. Estyn Evans suggested, 'It serves no useful purpose other than as a slippery short-cut to the summits.'

The Mourne mountain-scape is made up of steep heathery slopes, boulders of granite and the rocky tors, interspersed with rivers and woodlands. Stone lookout towers on the summits are places of shelter on wet days, their slopes strewn with angular blocks. I have walked these mountains, and many other Irish ones, on numerous occasions. For me, mountains embolden the imagination, and this evening there is a painterly quality to the landscape. The Mournes are also a place of valued memories. In 1977 I completed a traverse of the hills as part of the popular Mourne Wall Walk, an annual event in which several thousand hikers took part, but which was stopped in 1984 because of the damage being caused to the drystone wall.

***

In our final few weeks back in the woods, the chestnut and beech trees are heavy with leafage that looks harsh and splintery. There is a tired and stagnant feel to the grounds, an oppressive lazy stickiness is in the air. This period is referred to by gardeners as the 'August colour gap', since many of the plants that provided intense radiance during spring and summer have finished. It is also helped by my inescapable melancholy, a combination of missing the dazzling colours and the fact that the crescent silhouette of swifts has departed back to central and southern Africa. However, I can now safely say that mine eyes have seen the glory of the coming (and the going) of the swifts.

From tree to tree, other avifauna is on the move around the grounds, including wrens and woodpigeons. A juvenile song thrush, looking like a lost waif, makes a guest appearance on the forest floor opposite our cottage. The dumpy bird, which may weigh no more than thirty grams, with his speckled breast, is uncertain about his bearings. Over the course of six consecutive mornings and afternoons the small bird launches regular food forays from a nest in the hedge. With his delicately short, wiry legs, he is still learning the ropes but has mastered the art of pecking and poking, straying onto a longer grassy patch. His curiosity gets the better of him, twisting his neck and turning and swivelling his head, the bird drinks in the surroundings. A shrill squeak is repeated twice as he shyly wanders around soft leaves, unfazed by insects. At one point, with a meal on his mind, a pigeon eyes the young fledgling, quickly losing interest when I rush over with a brush. We are so taken with the bird that in honour of our location we nickname him 'Monty', and when his friend turns up we decide to call her 'Alto'.

The blackbirds are moulting, or at least lying low, but during our last week, robins start to sing as they begin establishing breeding territories. Blue tits, which have been acquiring new plumage, are noisy again with their thin sibilant calls. They feed on ripe elderberries and aphids, searching out beechnuts along paths, their brilliant blue caps giving off ultraviolet light which other blue tits can detect. Around the grounds, pruning, clipping, weeding and mowing is underway. In the surrounding hedges, burdock, ragwort and bindweed are burgeoning, but in several cases the seed heads of wilting plants are brown, with tatty leaves starting to change colour, their stems stiffening.

At the end of August, darkness is creeping into the woodland around 8 p.m. and summer has shot its bolt. Nights are growing colder and it is time for us to take our leave. But a part of me wants to remain in this sylvestral spot, so it is a pensive time of reflection. It is accurate to say that we have developed a fondness for the reality of our surroundings. It has been an exceptional experience and one that will not be erased easily from our minds, nor is it likely to be repeated. Having drunk deep on the wildlife of the estate, renting a patch of it as a tenant was a rare privilege and the fringe benefits were priceless. We look back on a bewitching twelve-month experience in which we were privy to a covert world, somewhere to cherish soothingly special but often fleeting moments. Full focus, we experienced nature on display, feeling the extreme force of the weather. We learned of the comings and goings of woodland creatures, witnessed the drama of the blackbird against the worm, the spider at odds with the fly, the boxing hares and scampering squirrels. The 'Montalto months' were a tranquil time when we basked in simple pleasures, the exotic and the quixotic. Part of our lives was spent in proximity to nature and wood-wandering, deriving delight in the ordinary and the everyday. For a year we were surrounded by the singing, croaking, mating and howling of varied species, all cheek by jowl in an open-air theatre.

Previously unknown dimensions of our temporary environment were uncovered. As guests, we were humble observers, indulging in spiritual renewal through the colour and light, the company of trees and the gossip of the forest, appreciating Mother Nature and her entanglements at her most serene and most severe. We looked at the world anew and with different eyes. It brought an understanding of the rhythms and hierarchies of the countryside, the speed of the passing seasons, and heart-stopping moments that have stayed long in my memory. Sightings of wildlife and magical vignettes of nature enriched it; not just the long-tailed tits or blackbirds, but goldfinches and song thrushes, their movements indelibly imprinted on my mind. I am confident that in any bird identity parade, armed with binoculars, I could select a gallery of the main suspects from among them. The sensory stimulation I experienced from sharing the same neighbourly space has led to an ornithological epiphany.

My journal is filled with the birds seen throughout the year, amounting to more than fifty species that were knitted into the fabric of daily life. Many details stand out: the stutter of the goldcrest, the shrill cry of the demented wren as it trickles about in the hedges, and not forgetting that master of concealment, the treecreeper. Birding is often filled with transcendental moments and the famed encounters of meaning, but it also brings an awareness that nature has an undiminished capacity to surprise. Some of my best moments were linked to my grandstand seat, part of a snapshot of that soundscape. While there was no shortage of drama, there was also a peacefulness from living in our own densely wooded pocket, which brought troughs in the sounds of the birds, days of quiet and days of noise, days of random wingbeats and low frequency calls. The geophony – the noise of the environment – made us familiar with the effect of wind, storms in the trees and woods, heavy rain and thunder, and water-flow.

Living here taught me that communing with nature involves hours of patience and stillness but brings rich rewards. Calming doses of it every so often help our overthinking minds. We revelled in the minutiae of woodland life and realised how fortunate we were to have shared that time with those creatures. It engendered a sense of well-being and nourishing small moments of wonder. We reflect on the satisfying unpredictability of a year of knowing that we have seen what most people miss out on, learning something of the signs, scents and sounds of the wild.

Spending time in Montalto brought an understanding of nature, our relationship to it and the constancy of change. Birding can be esoteric, but if I learned anything, it was to be continuously attentive and not to rush my walks or cycles. The old ways are the slow ways. If you properly wish to see birds then you must decelerate and concentrate, waiting for them to appear. I think of an analogy with buses: they do not wait for you, you wait for them. The American writer Barry Lopez had a simple credo: 'To be patient, to pay attention to the world that is not yourself, is the first step in the neophyte's discovery of the larger world outside the self, the landscape in which wisdom itself abides.' We valued the lack of noise, which provided a refuge from city life. They were softer sounds that I experienced: the thrush's trill, listening to the emotion in a blackbird's call, the swish of leaves and wind in the trees. Compare this with the harsher sounds of Belfast during the final years of the Troubles in the early 1990s: bombs and controlled explosions, the drone of nightly helicopters, the whine of military Land Rovers, police and ambulance sirens, the clamour and bustle of traffic – never mind the argumentative politicians.

By early September we have reached the last rites of summer with dropping temperatures. Conkers are falling from trees frayed at the edges and with a washed-out look; leaves are drooping, and the sun is lacking any warmth. This brings a seasonal circularity to our year of woodland life. Even with all the birding conversations on which I eavesdropped, I am still unable to say with certainty what they were talking about. Albert Camus declared autumn a 'second spring', where 'every leaf is a flower'. Flora names continue to throw up surprises and on a final 'gratitude' walk we come across the multiple flowers of pale-blue five-petalled forget-me-nots (*Myosotis arvensis*). In his poem 'The Keepsake', Samuel Taylor Coleridge popularised the name forget-me-not, which he found in a German folktale. In many countries it is symbolic of true love and memory.

'September sadness symptoms' cause a sense of heaviness to creep over us, stemming from summer's end and our imminent departure. Listless days are again in retreat and the colour balance of trees and plants is shifting. Long-distance migrants have gone, but two tits are trying to outdo each other: a coal tit with its loud and repetitive piping *see-too-see-too* competes with a blue tit's *tse-tse-tse-tsit*. On our last day, an unexpected September mist hangs motionless over the grounds. I attune myself to the silence on a serene walk around and the absence of traffic sounds, sirens and helicopters for one last time. Now we must take our own flight path, and the removal van arrives at high noon to empty Lakeside

Cottage and its adjoining sheds of our belongings. There is still a clarity to the light, but mornings are chilly, with a wistfulness to the speech of birds, although I am sure I overhear two blackbirds chinking a farewell benediction, tally-ho-ing us off as we seek fresh pastures.

Part III

Montalto *Resurgam*

Reawakening the Woods

'Whatever evaluation we finally make of a stretch of land, no matter how profound or accurate, we will find it inadequate. The land retains an identity of its own, still deeper and more subtle than we can know. Our obligation towards it then becomes simple: to approach with an uncalculating mind, with an attitude of regard. To try to sense the range and variety of its expression, its weather and colour and animals. To intend from the beginning to preserve some of the mystery within it as a kind of wisdom to be experienced, not questioned. And to be alert for its opening, for that moment when something sacred reveals itself within the mundane, and you know the land knows you are there.'

Barry Lopez, *Arctic Dreams*

By the summer of 2024, six years after the Montalto estate opened its gates to the public, the revitalising changes made to the grounds are immediately apparent. On a July morning, as

I approach from The Spa, now the main entry point, large stands of purple rhododendron line the winding route, speed restrictions with ramps and CCTV cameras are in place, while signs warn: 'Slow: red squirrels'. In the surrounding sloping fields, a hardy flock of Herdwick sheep grazes peacefully, while other land is let to farmers for silage-making. During the second decade of the twenty-first century the grounds were radically reimagined, and on this, my first visit in more than thirty years, it is difficult to find my bearings. Although the layout of the main roads is similar, there has been an unimaginable rejuvenation of plants and trees, and it is easy to lose myself in the new foliage, flora and vegetation. To quote Rilke, 'Each step a new arrival.'

It is also hard to decide where to go and which trail to take, since around every corner there is a dynamic and vigorous energy to the grounds tended by a team of gardeners and foresters. During our time, the woodlands were forsaken and had fallen into decay. Now the rough and ready has been smoothed away, shabby has become chic where new soft mulch paths lead to unfamiliar gardens, woods and groves; each bend gives rise to a satisfying prospect. Everywhere I look in the flourishing regrowth, there is something tangible and aesthetically pleasing: azalea beds here, a wildflower meadow there, glowing spectacles of pink, blue and white hydrangeas, a pergola, folly or a curious piece of outdoor sculpture. As well as the colours and artwork, there is a sensory side, with *Cercidiphyllum japonicum*, more commonly called katsura trees, releasing a delicious caramel and burnt sugar smell near the main house. In another area, *Edgeworthia chrysantha* 'Grandiflora', a bushy deciduous shrub with fragrant yellow flowers opens from hairy buds, while sweet-scented viburnums, with their distinctive white and pink blooms, fill the summer air with heady aromatic fragrance. On a light breeze, and from clusters of the pink-flowering Abelia, I detect a sweet perfume aroma similar to jasmine.

Thirty years in the life of a forest is nothing, but it is clear to me from wandering hither and thither with my ears, eyes and nose wide open, that not only does Montalto have a fresh bouquet, it also has a new mojo and mantra: 'Reconnect with nature. Slow down and take comfort in the natural beauty around you.' Scrubby growth has disappeared, neglected forests have been brought back to life and thousands of trees introduced in a woodland that has been startlingly reshaped. *Rhododendron ponticum*, which is a weed, has been replaced by *Rhododendron arboreum*, the showy red-flower tree rhododendron, as well as by other species and varieties. The ambience is enhanced with the woodland perennials *actaea*, the decorative flowering *auriculas*, and the heart-shaped leaves of the delicate spreading *omphalodes*. Between the paths and copses of trees and shrubs, magnolia, ferns and the handsome *cornus*, deciduous trees and small shrubs commonly known as dogwood, now prosper.

While the estate may have become commodified and commercialised, the Wilson family has lavished love and imagination on the grounds, with the creation of artfully crafted walking trails, stretching from the Ballynahinch River up Ednavady Hill, and areas in between. Individually themed gardens covering the seasons cater for a variety of horticultural tastes: fern garden, winter garden, alpine garden, walled garden, a rock garden and a secret garden. There is even a lost garden that has been unearthed and restored. As I cross the grass at the front of the house, I immerse myself in a velvety weed-free experience. Close by stand large beds of *Buxus sempervirens*, common box, and a mature topiary laurel umbrella, *Prunus lusitanica*, with dark green glossy leaves.

However, the gardeners working here have little time to breathe in their surroundings and rest on their topiary laurels – although *Laurus nobilis*, the aromatic evergreen tree and large shrub, is widespread. On a walk through the long-standing Donkey Pad – a route taken in olden days by those making deliveries – I come across a statue of two woodcutters carved from fallen oak trees, sitting on a log, looking pleased with their lot. Commissioned by the owners, they were created by a local artist specialising in wood carving, and in the spring the statue is surrounded by bluebells. I test one of the wooden benches, teleporting myself to the forget-me-not memories and moments of transcendence from more than thirty summers ago that come flooding back. If anything sums up the *genius loci* for me, birdsong brings an intense feeling of connection with the land, trees and countryside.

Birds still have the freedom of the Montalto skies, but on a variety of walks between July and October 2024, they are much harder to see. There may be a number of reasons for the absence of the chirruping of songsters that we enjoyed, yet I neither caught sight of, nor heard, finches, tits, robins or thrushes, although birdcall ringtones are audible. On busy days, hundreds of visitors with their families are spread around the grounds, while dogs are prevalent and a bark park has been created; along with increased footfall, park-runs and numerous other events, all this may collectively have contributed to a decrease in birdlife. Undeniably, the early 1990s' tranquillity that we enjoyed during our stay has mutated into a much more cacophonous environment. Blackbirds, one of the lead vocalists of the spring dawn chorus, have largely disappeared, although this is symptomatic of a wider picture, where they have, in general, left woodlands and are now more commonly found in suburban gardens.

However, although it is a transformed birding scene and there appear to be fewer flying from tree to tree, it is by no means a gloomy picture of ornithological decline, as a fresh birdwatching dimension has been added. Courtship still has a hold in the woods and new birds have taken over. In the early spring a loud drumming can be heard echoing around the woods, a sign that birds are busy building their nests. The noise of this bird – the great spotted woodpecker – with its machine-gun resonance during springtime breeding displays, and loud and strident *kik-kik* call, was not heard in Montalto nor anywhere in Ireland during the 1990s but has now increased its spread to every county. The species recolonised Ireland in 2005 and the first breeding pair was discovered in County Down the following year. Known to birders as 'great spots' or the 'greater pecker', the woodpecker arrived on the Montalto estate in 2017 and returned to the same tree the following year, where it made a new nest. Part of the thrill of the woodpecker is not necessarily about seeing the bird but about hearing it. A tapping sound means it is digging out a nest hole in a tree trunk with its beak and the birds make a new hole each year, which is wide at the bottom to make room for chicks. Although I did not witness it at first hand, those who have seen it speak of its distinctive bouncing flight and the fact that it spends most of its time climbing tree trunks or perching. The birds have been spotted, with their pied black-and-white plumage and distinctive red neck or head markings, in various parts of the estate: the bird feeder outside the ticket office, and in oak trees and on fence posts. By 2024 at least three breeding pairs have set up home in the environs and are fond of stripping the bark of Spanish chestnut trees.

Other new settlers have also made their way into the grounds since our sojourn. Jays, part of the corvid family, arrived around 2015. Noted for their raucous squawk, several dozen of them have been seen with their white flash zipping through the woods. Buzzards have expanded their territories since the 1990s, setting up home in Montalto's tall treetops, while another breeding newcomer is the raven. Right on cue, on one of my visits a buzzard pops up in a mature oak tree, allowing me long enough to be aware of its size. I am surprised that the bird is a small-looking predator, but it is keeping a close eye on pigeons – although they could well be a level or two above its 'prey' grade. Sightings have been reported of red kites, graceful birds of prey, which may have been passing through on their way elsewhere. The flash of a kingfisher has been noted along the Ballynahinch River, as well as dippers, while tree-dwelling pine martens, known in Irish as the *cat crainn* (tree cat), are part of Montalto's new animal kingdom.

Throughout Ireland the Covid-19 pandemic led to an increase in recreational birdwatching, with more people than ever taking their binoculars for a walk. There is now a growing body of evidence that links our physical and mental health with the time we spend outdoors. In 2024 an American study showed that just thirty minutes spent birdwatching can send our spirits soaring, benefit mental fatigue and help lower blood pressure. Academics from North Carolina State University claimed that researchers randomly assigned to a group watching birds saw greater improvements in their well-being compared with those assigned to a nature-walking group. Not only does it bring enhanced enjoyment of the ordinary, but it also provides moments of high drama and memories to last a lifetime. Nature may be repetitious but it is never boring, and during our time living in Lakeside Cottage we were made aware of its transcendent power to comfort, move and inspire.

Birds continue to populate my mind and imagination. I did not realise it then, but living in Montalto taught me how to look at birds and butterflies, observing them closely in an unhurried way – even though some of them hurried away – and to concentrate on the wonders of nature. In the intervening years there has been a surge of interest in the place of birds in human culture and of the way in which they have become encoded in our lives. By the mid-2020s a wander through the woods has metamorphosed into 'forest bathing', based on the ancient Japanese practice of *shinrin-yoku*. This principle encourages walkers to experience nature through smell, touch, hearing and taste, as well as sight, coupled with mindfulness. Some visitors on a leisurely stroll are indulging in what is referred to as an 'awe walk', which involves marvelling at nature. And at the end of one of my walks, my spirits are 'awesomely' heartened by the sight of two active speckled wood butterflies with their distinctive wing eye spots in a small pool of sunlight. It is a butterfly with which I first became familiar in Montalto during our stay, and it is a pleasure to find that it still enjoys a prolonged browse on bushes here.

***

Constructed from a fallow field in 2019, the fruit garden was designed by June Wilson. A path leads me past plum and mulberry trees, skirts a wildflower meadow and an orchard with heritage trees, such as 'The Apple Blood of the Boyne' and the fragrant 'Cavan Wine Apple' with its delicate pink blushes. This links to the *pièce de résistance*, the lost garden. The *resurgam* of this garden represents for me one of the most compelling stories in the restoration of the grounds. As its name implies, it was forsaken until a cascade of discoveries in 2018 led to gardeners unearthing a long-forgotten area that was riotously overrun with weeds and smothered in vegetation. It was recreated five years later and requires a great deal of maintenance. Entrance to the garden is through a pair of gates, which themselves were lost to the devouring trunks of two large conifers. Curious artefacts and original features were uncovered. Staff worked with a historic gardens consultant to put together the pieces of the jigsaw, bringing the sunken garden back to life and exposing it to view for the first time in more than eighty years. A stroll around the undulating paths showcases an understanding of how the historic setting would have looked when the Clanwilliam family was in residence. The garden is south-facing and sheltered, which is the reason the Victorian glasshouse is located here – the ideal place for fruits needing a warm and humid climate to help lengthen the growing season.

A replica of the rose arbour, found in a state of disrepair, was designed and created by an engineer, placed within its original setting and planted with climbing roses that include the pleasing perfume of the pink and apricot blooms of the pirouette rose. Clearing of the site uncovered a stone bench seat alongside part of the garden wall. A large stone stag has been placed beside original metal fencing symbolising that the estate once had a deer park adjacent to the lost garden. More recently, feral deer have been seen roaming in the locality and are thought to be the descendants of 'escapers' from Montalto's original herd.

The lost garden path that I follow snakes back and forth over streams with new timber, arriving into the restored rock garden with raised alpine beds, colourful displays and numerous pot plants. The remains of two bridges, linking one side of the garden to the other, have been reinstated in a similar design to their original settings. With, in my opinion, a different vibe from the rest of the estate, the garden blends quiet, shady sections with light-splashed open areas. Shrubs such as the mock orange philadelphus and the shiny-leaved mahonia, as well as native trees that had seeded, providing a canopy, were discovered. As I walk through this serene garden, plants that are easy on the eye include asplenium, camellia and brunnera. It is a location where I reflect on the hand of history, which, like nature, moves in cycles. This is, I determine, a wistful place to sit and listen carefully; you may hear echoes of bygone days as you drink in the flower-fest of the present in a bucolic setting with a touch of nostalgia where soothing water trickles under bridges.

One part of the garden contains the restored glasshouse used to decorate a fern bed. The hot house was kept humid using evaporated water and was where exotic and tender equatorial plants were protected. Abandoned pipes now sit alongside the remains of a tall brick spine wall that divided the glasshouse from the boiler house, potting shed and store. These ancient and decaying relics are the detritus of a previous horticultural incarnation. A sepia snapshot of how it looked is on display, offering a portal into the past and a glimpse of long-forgotten lives. Embedded within them is a beguiling and historic industrial aura reflecting a feat of engineering, which is now in startling contrast with the colourful growth of a lost garden that has healed itself.

***

Woods do not stay the same forever, but in a period of just over thirty years striking changes have taken place. Aside from the establishment of gardens and trails, thousands of trees have been planted. With map in hand, and on a meandering roam around the woods, I stumble on acers, deciduous azaleas and vines, all taking their place alongside established beech, birch, lime, Douglas fir, oak and sycamore. Newly layered tree plantations include two of four remaining champion trees: liquidambar and sycamore. The two others are a redwood sequoia and a black pine. During one recent winter, root-balled or bareroot trees from a nursery were introduced. Species such as variegated beech, sweet chestnut, hornbeam and blue cedar, some of which produce colour during specific times of the year, are part of the woodland thicket.

From speaking to foresters and gardeners in the estate, it is a pleasure to learn that the science and art of caring for trees and plants, known as arboriculture, has taken on a new twenty-first-century meaning. Forest etiquette demands that trees in the grounds are now surveyed every year and beeches that are diseased are removed for health and safety reasons. In specific instances the foresters reduce the weight of the crown; in another a beech has been left standing, resembling a totem pole normally found in the US or Canada, creating a habitat for wildlife. On 24 January 2025, Storm Éowyn blasted its way across Ireland, destroying hundreds of thousands of mature trees in numerous woodlands. The most ferocious storm in living memory, it affected every part of the Montalto estate, with hundreds of trees brought down and extensive damage in many areas. Veteran oaks, in some cases 200 years old, and 150-year-old beech trees, were among the casualties in a trail of destruction that left a palpable sense of bereavement, as well as resulting in a longer-term effect on biodiversity.

As part of the continuing programme of stability and maintenance, support is provided for older trees. For a creaking sycamore – one of the estate's oldest trees – gardeners have installed steel rods, acting as a brace to take the weight of the sagging branches, strengthen the tree and lessen the threat of potential damage during severe weather. Around the grounds large sculpted spheres have been placed. These were created from rusted steel by a local artist and metalworker Damian Cooper. One is welded into a large oak tree, while another is mounted on the stump of a blue spruce that fell during Storm Ophelia in 2017. Others are near the boathouse, where two are high in the bough of a beech tree and another is positioned on a tree stump at the winter garden. One of the tree-mounted spheres is made of used rusted metal horseshoes, giving the effect of a beechnut.

One of the favourite locations where I enjoyed lingering during our stay in Montalto, the Low Wood, remains largely untouched by time, though a small part of it has now become a classic example of chaos turned into order, and then chaos again, since one section is a clamorous children's play area. The wood, which had been allowed to run wild, has undergone a remarkable transformation, and part of it has been reinvented as an adventure park with a pond, climbing tower, slides and a coffee cabin. The jungle-style atmosphere of fallen or distressed trees, gnarled and twisted and decayed stumps, along with masses of overgrown weeds and briers, has been swept away. Larch trees, with a dangerous fungus-like disease *Phytophthora ramorum*, were cut down, and laurel and rhododendron cleared. A quiet, untrodden place, the wood had long been neglected and ash trees were removed by experts because of ash dieback, where an invasive fungus kills the trees. Since the early 1990s natural regeneration has taken place, but there has also been fresh planting of oak, birch, alder and beech.

However, the Low Wood has not been completely tamed. One large section has been allowed to continue its spread in a carnival of wild greenery running close to the Ballynahinch River and, with fewer visitors in this part of the wood, it has retained its enchanting otherworldly feel of disorderliness. Nature has evolved and ramrod-straight trees, including some of those that I leaned against, have added a noticeable increase to their girth; others have aged gracefully, though their skin is wrinkling, while some loners, with advancing years and mossy growths, appear to have eclipsed their 'youthfulness'. Tree crowns are thinning, which leads me to a comparison with my own 'up top' hair, no longer growing in the way it did in more youthful times.

By the mid-2020s the selfie-stick TikTokers and Instagram-mers are active. Nowadays a raft of AI-assisted tools, photo recognition apps such as LeafSnap and PlantNet can identity shrubs, flowers and trees at the click of a button, while 1,001 other apps provide on-the-spot birdsong recognition. In the tap of an app, we can all become instant woodlanders. However, not all identifications are correct; some apps are woefully inaccurate and misidentify plants or birds. An ornithological friend of mine likes to call them 'Pain in the apps'. I rewind to more than thirty years earlier, when the technological landscape was completely different. In the early 1990s 'tweets' were bird calls, 'spam' was something in a can, a 'mac' was a raincoat, and a cloud was a fluffy mass of droplets. It was a time before YouTube, social media, iPads, smartphones, chatbox and Snapchats and the all-conquering tech Goliaths of Google and Apple.

In days of yore, a drone was a male bee but now is better known as an unmanned aerial vehicle used to take photographs from the air, while worms can delete computer files and AI is no longer just farm speak for artificial insemination in animals. The prevalence of screens serves as a reminder of the work of Wendell Berry, the poet laureate of America's farmland, and of his 1960s collection *The Peace of Wild Things*: 'Breathe with unconditional breath / the unconditioned air. / Shun electric wire. / Communicate slowly. Live / a three-dimensioned life; / stay away from screens. / Stay away from anything / that obscures the place it is in.' Around the lake, a giant green sward of the leaves of the bog plant gunnera, a heavyweight of the perennials and now regarded as an invasive species, continues to thrive, appearing to have spread with more dramatic effect. Lilies and yellow flag iris bring colour, while acers, including Japanese maples, and sweet chestnut fan out around the boathouse where a large weeping willow takes advantage of the damp, moist soil. The lake itself has not changed in size but is now abustle with activity. Through my binoculars I watch swans, mallard, coots and teal glide slowly, along with crested and little grebes; for the first time moorhens have built a nest beside the lake.

And what of our temporary home where we spent our year in the woods? The former Lakeside Cottage has been reinvented as an office and toilet block, now fulfilling the role of answering the call of nature. Only the roof and chimney pot remain untouched. At one side of the building, tall purple stands of verbena grow alongside scented, soft, lime-green blooms of lady's mantle with its fan-shaped leaves. The wall of the stable block where we stored our furniture is adorned with Boston ivy. The path leading from the cottage to the mansion and lake was one of our favourite strolls; now long stems of the billowing flaming-red flowers of crocosmia set the borders alight, their heads dancing in the wind. At the front of the main house is a lawn, along with a formal garden with a defined structure and geometric shape, which has been planted to replicate the appearance of the house's famed ballroom. A display of nepeta produces a profusion of lavender-blue flowers. Along a shady garden path, the dark red hanging bells of fuchsia bestow summer colour. During one of my visits, these small thimbles of fuchsia are a haven for the contented humming of honeybees and fluffy, gingery carder bumblebees.

Leading up through a cathedral of tall uniform pines and overarching laurel branches, the history trail rises to the story-haunted Ednavady Hill where the spirit of 1798 is flourishing. Steel cut-out figures resemble the United Irish rebels with their long pikes. Crown soldiers are hiding in the woods beside tree stumps, while others assume crouched firing positions at the site of the Battle of Ballynahinch. Echoes of the past are all around in a walk through time. The large sloping hill, an open patch of wide, steep grassland was the headquarters of the rebels' encampment, although it extended even farther and has since been developed with housing and a primary school. Today the occupants of Ednavady are grazing Cheviots, black-faced Suffolk and the black-nosed Dutch Texel breed of sheep, enclosed by thick tree cover on all sides. A wooden fence surrounds the field where a shepherdess and an affable sheepdog are busy looking after their flock. One of the sheep gives me an inquisitive look before performing an upside-down stretching exercise. Their bleating mixes with the shouts and screams of children playing outdoors at the adjacent primary school.

From this vantage point, the vista stretches across Ballynahinch and the surrounding countryside. Known as the five-counties view, the wider lie of the land remains remarkably authentic. Even since our stay, the scenic landscape may have changed little, but the agricultural world has gone through a seismic shift. Uber-neat and kempt hedges dominate the roadsides, while monoculture farming is based on growing only one type of crop at one time on a specific field or breeding only one species of animal on a farm. Italian ryegrass is grown and boosted by fertiliser, which means it thrives quickly and requires cutting five or six times a year, whereas three decades ago it was cut once. The views from Ednavady embrace new housing developments and satellite dishes, with the presence of pylons, phone masts and wind turbines dotting the mid-Down terrain. As I stand here and look out across Ednavady Hill, it is clear, though, that there is an emotional link to the landscape for many people in the mid-Down area. Today, historic names live on in the town in the form of Lord Moira Park and Clanwilliams Court.

Farther along the history trail and a short distance from Ednavady, masses of ferns and wood sorrel line the route that leads me to a rath, or ringfort, common in Ireland during the early medieval period from AD 500–1100 and occupied by successful farmers. The site, now overgrown with trees and foliage, is believed to have been home to a small community or an extended family with two dwellings or roundhouses. A nearby enclosure was thought to have been used for livestock, surrounded by a bank and ditch which provided protection against natural predators and cattle raids. An area of raised ground connecting the two features holds a linear bank and ditches on either side.

It may be an exaggeration to say that more than thirty years after our time here, I am still living in the afterglow of those months. Ambling around the restored grounds, finding out about the trails and much more feels surreal, as though bumping into my thirty-something self, but in unaccustomed surroundings. Part of me still resides in the estate, contemplating four seasons of woodland reflection. The Welsh language has a word for this, *cynefin*, meaning one's biological cultural, geographic and spiritual haunt or a habitat that has become a touchstone. With my muscle memory, I reflect on the changes, recalling specific sites that transfixed us. We had looked with newly opened eyes, and the words of the gamekeeper about the small, natural wonders stay with us forever. A smorgasbord of snapshot moments still gleams brightly in the tutelar spirit of the woods intimately linked to our time there: the bouncy, undulating flight of goldfinches, scampering squirrels, high-speed hares, slow-moving treecreepers, parties of long-tailed tits, and the smell of the sap of pine – not forgetting the leaf-litter, fallen trees, stormy nights and snowfalls.

***

While the climate emergency has cast a long shadow over many countries and is causing confusion for animals, insects, trees and plants, the regeneration of Montalto and physical changes to the grounds represent an exceptional development. The estate believes in sustainability: rainwater is harvested, native trees are planted, pollinator flowers enhance the gardens, the use of pesticides has been reduced, and fallen branches are turned into woodchip to help control weeds. But a considerable amount of hand-weeding is still necessary, involving a mixture of people power as well as mulch.

In an anxious world where numerous aspects of natural life are struggling with global warming, retreating glaciers and extreme weather, Montalto may be viewed as a symbol of hope with a nature-focused atmosphere. People come here to escape from the artificial noise, to tune into wildlife and natural sounds. As part of the bigger picture, a new world is emerging, with Europe warming faster than the global average. Exceptional temperatures with a spate of intense heatwaves have brought thunderstorms, tornadoes, cyclones and raging wildfires set off by extreme drought, while coastal erosion and rampaging floods are causing havoc.

There are many threats to the earth's future, with climate change firmly taking hold. In Britain butterfly numbers have fallen by one-third since 2000. European figures show species that were previously the most abundant have decreased on average by 8 per cent each year, while the number for all species is much higher, at about 15 per cent. Bumblebees are intolerant of heat and their numbers too have shrunk throughout Europe as temperatures continue to rise.

Every week brings record-breaking weather extremes and according to Met Éireann, based on records going back 125 years, 2024 was the warmest year on record by a wide margin for Ireland, with indications that the years to follow will be even warmer. In 2023, for the first time, Ireland's annual average temperature was greater than eleven degrees Celsius. It was also the third wettest since records began at Armagh Observatory in 1795.

Many wider-world events are affecting Ireland and there is little doubt that global warming has blurred the edges of seasons here and upset the natural order. The unpredictable, capricious and much-maligned Irish weather has long been a source of conversation and scrutiny. However, the shifting weather patterns, particularly with wetter and warmer temperatures in more recent years, are upsetting the regular rhythm of the seasons, causing stress to wildlife and making it more susceptible to pests and disease. Nature is being assaulted from every angle. For all its lush greenery and reputation as the 'Emerald Isle', Ireland is now one of the most nature-depleted European countries. There has been a huge loss of up to 90 per cent of wetlands, more than anywhere else, and with just over 10 per cent of native tree cover, Ireland has the lowest cover in Europe.

The town of Downpatrick, south of Ballynahinch, suffered unprecedented flooding at the end of 2023 after intense storms. Fifty businesses were swamped when the overflowing Quoile River burst its banks in the wettest October on record. Shops and businesses were destroyed by the flooding and structural defects led to the bulldozing of a supermarket. Nearby, Portadown and Newry also suffered serious flooding. During that winter, the ferocious weather presented a freshly named storm each week.

One of the biggest natural-world differences between the 1990s and the 2020s is the reduction in the number of bugs, which are at the foundation of the food chain. Known as the 'insect apocalypse', this has led to Ireland's bugs, bees and butterflies disappearing at an alarming rate. The depletion is attributed to agricultural intensification and habitat loss in flower-rich meadows, which has had a major impact on food and nesting sites for insects. There is less space for wild bees and a raft of bugs, grasshoppers, wasps, butterflies, moths and soldier beetles, nicknamed 'bloodsuckers'. Scientists refer to this as the 'shifting baseline syndrome'. Effectively, it is a gradual change in the accepted normal condition of the natural environment due to a lack of knowledge of previous information or a lack of experience.

Entomologists believe that of the 100 species of native bees in Ireland, one-third are threatened with extinction. Sourcing pollen and nesting sites has become harder for wild bees, and they are finding themselves starving and homeless in a changed landscape. The dearth of insects has manifested itself in diverse ways. In the 1990s, if we ate al fresco or organised barbecues, we could be sure of a marching army of ants appearing, but this is no longer the case.

The decrease in insect numbers and the change in landscape has become obviously apparent to me as someone who has spent a considerable amount of time on the road researching and writing books. In the 1980s and 1990s a 400-mile drive from west Cork to Belfast took at least six hours along twisting country roads, or what Fodor's Guide likes to label 'Supernarrow B roads'. Butterflies cartwheeled over the windscreen of the car, which became splattered with a variety of bees, wasps, ants, ladybirds, flies and moths, but now insects rarely blur my vision. Frequently, owing to 'the windshield phenomenon', I had to stop the car to wash the windscreen, as well as scraping the number plate and headlights, which attracted a blizzard of moths. More than forty years on, in the mid-2020s, and in a journey that now takes under five hours, much of it on motorways, there is no need to stop for the 'splat test'. For example, on a return journey from the Burren in County Clare in summer 2024, only two insects met their end on the windscreen of our car. It may be an unscientific survey, but it highlights the reality of the precarious plight of our six-legged fellow earth-dwellers.

Butterflies are in free fall, yet another sign of the changing face of the Irish countryside, as their numbers continue to drop alarmingly. Data in 2024 suggests that, in total, 18 per cent of Ireland's native butterflies – a key indicator species – face extinction, and 15 per cent have nearly reached threatened status. The torrential rain and the use of neonicotinoid pesticides have been blamed for this disastrous fall in numbers. Since 2008 one of the most common of all, the green-veined white, has declined by 83 per cent, while others are experiencing reductions of around 67 per cent. Only one of Ireland's insects, the marsh fritillary butterfly, is listed under the EU's habitats directive, which contains measures to preserve wild flora and fauna, and even then, the protection provided by this is confined to only some parts of Ireland. In the North, a UK-wide wildlife survey, known as the Big Butterfly Count, recorded in summer 2024 a drop of 71 per cent in the number of butterflies spotted compared with the previous year. As a result, with these alluring winged insects said to be at their lowest ebb for fifty years, the Butterfly Conservation charity has declared a 'Butterfly Emergency'.

Another sobering statistic is that more than half of native Irish plant species have declined since 2004. The figure was revealed in the fourth National Biodiversity Action Plan released early in 2024, which is tackling some of Ireland's accelerating species loss. Botanical researchers also estimate that Irish plants now flower about a month earlier than they once did. Fertilisers reduce wildflower diversity, but some farmers are leaving flower-rich pasture and meadows in place rather than reseeding with less diverse grass. Attitudes have changed too, so that dandelions are now seen as being strikingly beautiful, bringing to life countless pollinators, birds and mammals – a contrast from a time not that long ago when gardeners held a bitter prejudice against them. 'Farming for Nature' ambassadors are helping the situation by reducing the use of fertilisers and chemicals, while gardeners throughout the country are cutting back on mowing their lawns to give wildflowers the opportunity to flourish as part of rewilding. Under-pampering is popular, allowing pockets of land to grow pollinator habitats, while 'No Mow May' – a month in which lawnmower duties are skipped – is for pollinators and lazy gardeners. Weeds too have been rehabilitated, with the farming community in parts of Ireland adopting a mindset-change to thistles, nettles and invasive plants.

Sixty per cent of Irish birds are either orange- or red-listed, meaning they are under threat, and adding to this headache is the fact that up to half of Ireland's rivers – where many birds thrive – are polluted. The traffic light register of red, orange and green indicates an increasing level of conservation concern and, as birdlife struggles with climate change, many species are faced with difficulties surviving. This health check shows that 63 per cent of

Ireland's native birds are at risk, including the hen harrier. Since 2002 their numbers have decreased rapidly and there is worry that the bird will face extinction. The land suitable for them to live has become rare, not just in Ireland but across Europe. By late 2024 there were around 100 breeding pairs left in Ireland. In Tyrone, in 2023, only nine out of a total of thirty-four territorial pairs were recorded in the county, with just one chick detected.

The changing face of agriculture in Ireland has resulted in a serious fall in the number of yellowhammers, which were much more numerous in the 1990s. Once a common sight in the mid-Down landscape, where mixed farming with cereal crops was widespread, the birds' winter food sources have been reduced with the drop in grain.

Since the 1970s the population of the curlew has fallen by a staggering 85 per cent, mostly through habitat loss, and by early 2024 there were just 100 breeding pairs left in Ireland. However, in the North by the autumn of that year, under the UK's Curlew LIFE project, numbers had seen a turnaround, with a steady increase in breeding pairs on Upper and Lower Lough Erne in County Fermanagh, and on the Antrim Plateau. Many other wading birds are in serious decline, but a ray of optimism emerged when in 2024 the National Parks and Wildlife Service (NPWS) and the Department of Agriculture in the Republic launched a €25-million wader breeding project to attempt to redress the situation. The project is a collaboration with other agencies and considers the dwindling numbers of redshank, lapwing, golden plover and snipe. The ambitious scheme involves plans to revive habitat loss by restoring traditional wet grasslands, helping with a captive breeding programme and protecting the waders from predators.

Another story of hope is the corncrake. For more than thirty years this species declined steadily, but in 2024 it was reported that there had been a 35 per cent increase in corncrake territories since 2019, with the restoration of large areas of peatlands in the midlands and County Mayo. Funding schemes are helping farmers focus on birdlife through nature-friendly agriculture. Under the Corncrake Farm Plan and Corncrake LIFE, farmers receive a financial reward from the NPWS. Thanks to this project, by 2024 the number of recorded corncrake territories stood at 233, the highest in twenty-five years, although it remains red-listed as a species with around 150 breeding pairs. In summer 2024 the corncrake was also heard in County Kerry for the first time in many decades, while in the same year great spotted woodpeckers started breeding in Killarney National Park.

Under the NPWS reintroduction programme, a number of ospreys, fish-eating birds of prey which are believed to have become extinct as breeding birds in Ireland 200 years ago, were released in Killarney. The NPWS also reintroduced white-tailed sea eagles, and although the species has experienced ups and downs, it is now much happier. In 2020 the NPWS launched the second phase of its reintroduction project, bolstering existing Irish numbers. By July that year a small breeding population of up to ten pairs of white-tailed sea eagles had successfully fledged thirty-one chicks across Munster and into Galway.

Ireland's gain has sometimes been at the expense of another country's loss. In January 2024 Sweden experienced its coldest weather for decades, resulting in a spillover of waxwings searching for food, in particular berries that grow widely in Irish rowan trees. On the positive side a number of birds have come to Irish shores, such as little egrets, while the mid-2020s have seen at least one extremely rare bird visit the country. In spring 2024 a North American bird turned up near Castlebar and stirred considerable excitement among birdwatchers who descended on the village of Belcarra. The yellow-crowned night heron, named for its habit of feeding between late evening and early morning, is thought to have been caught up in a hurricane system on the Florida coast, which blew it off course to County Mayo. There had been one previous sighting of the bird recorded in Europe, several years earlier, but this was the first time it had been spotted in Ireland. Since 2019 sightings have also been reported by ornithologists of a south polar skua – a large gull-like visitor which breeds in the Antarctic – while they were sea-watching off the south coast of Ireland. And in the early 2020s the European bee-eater, a bird that winters in Africa and makes its way to Spain, became disoriented, ending up on Dursey Island, off the Beara peninsula in west Cork.

It's not just the birdlife suffering. Climatic changes to regular seasons are causing hibernating animals, such as dormice, to wake up earlier, and making red deer rut later. Extinction threatens forty-eight species living in the Irish marine environment, including fish, crustaceans, shellfish and invertebrates. Fish from southern climes are visiting Irish waters; eels can no longer navigate the changing currents to reach their Sargasso Sea breeding grounds and salmon are disappearing at an alarming rate from rivers.

This book is not a call to arms (the cynic might say that we have had enough of those in Ireland in the past few centuries), but we are hurtling towards a nature emergency and biodiversity crisis in an increasingly fragile and fomented world. If you even glance at newspaper headlines, and listen to or watch the news, then it is a depressing picture of the natural world being assaulted from all sides. The Climate Change Advisory Council was formed in Ireland in 2015 to support the country's transition to a biodiversity-rich, environmentally sustainable and climate-neutral resilient society. While targets and plans have been initiated and a range of carbon-budget proposals up to 2035 calculated, representing the total amount of emissions that may be released, vital issues have not been addressed. Many conservationists and environmentalists believe that it is time to turn the tide. Critical work remains to be done to save, preserve and enhance our native species, and nature recovery should be tackled with greater urgency.

Despite all the doom and pessimism that surrounds the climate emergency, spending time in the woods, sitting, meditating or cogitating brings the balm of a 'nature pill' along with other benefits. Countless studies have confirmed that nature has a stress-busting effect and even a small amount of exposure to plants makes a significant difference and improves cognitive function. The link with nature during the Covid pandemic was a vital lifeline for many, frequently inducing a more positive emotional state.

Trees are also of crucial importance in the regulation of the climate, and in one small corner of the County Down countryside the loftiest redwood and the smallest plant play their part, providing enchantment all around, if we take the time to look and listen. Henry David Thoreau's summation is worth remembering: 'I went to the woods because I wished to live deliberately, to front only the essential facts of life, and see if I could not learn what it had to teach, and not, when I came to die to discover that I had not lived … I wanted to live deep and suck out all the marrow of life.'

Postscript

An Avian Odyssey

'I am friend to the pilibeen, the red-necked chough, the parsnip landrail, the pilibeen móna, the bottle-tailed tit, the common marsh-coot, the speckle-toed guillemot, the pilibeen sléibhe, the Mohar gannet, the peregrine plough-gull, the long-eared bush-owl, the Wicklow small-fowl, the bevil-beaked chough, the hooded tit, the pilibeen uisce, the common corby, the fish-tailed mud-piper, the crúiskeen lawn, the carrion sea-cock, the green-lidded parakeet, the brown bog-martin, the maritime wren, the dove-tailed wheatcrake, the beaded daw, the Galway hill-bantam and the pilibeen cathrach.'

Flann O'Brien, *At Swim-Two-Birds*

If I close my eyes and cast my mind back over more than thirty years, I can recall hearing and seeing my totem birds, and instantly I am back in a 'Montalto moment' as they trigger memories. The year living there was stored in a corner of my mind for decades and the experience of the fierce storms and dawn chorus frequently drifts back. As well as being a stimulant to the senses, spending time there led to an ornithological eruption for me. Previously, the common birds were known to me, but others came under the term LBJ: Little Brown Jobs. Having lived in three cities for varying periods, Montalto was an epiphany. I learned how to espy the creatures of the air by taking the time to seek out the birds, which was instrumental in moving me along my personal bird-watching odyssey.

For a year I had communed cheek-to-beak with birds, some of whom became super-heroes, their songs adding a gracefulness to the air. Looking back, the cumulative experience was filled with glimpses, shapeshifting memories and partial views. Living in Montalto created an appetite for exploring the wider Irish birding world – and farther afield – and has been a wellspring for my writing, which is at the intersection of nature, people and history. My time there dealt mostly with the woodland variety but opened up a broader sphere, with the opportunity to go on trips to watch birds at home and abroad.

Soaring through streets, swirling around parks and gardens, fields and farmyards, and in rivers and mountains, birds became the soundtrack to my travels. The allure of watching them held me in thrall. After our time in the cottage, I went on to write five travel books about Ireland and to research information for a variety of international guidebooks to the country, as well as working for tourism agencies, newspapers, magazines and websites. All this led to intermittent roaming around the country, visiting each county and little-known places. At the risk of becoming a bird nerd, I made it a principle of my writing to seek out varied species. Frequently, birds were an aside to the main quest, but they were also a bridge linking journeys interspersed with interviews and local fact-finding. Amidst my foot-slogging, travel by two wheels and four, and note-taking, birds often took centre stage as serendipitous sightings.

The birds formed part of the subtle sources of memories and moods as I micro-explored different regions. They became the essence of a warm summer day or a freezing weekend in December. Geographically, Ireland may not be large, but looking back at my travelling and writing throughout the different regions of the country brings to mind what I have heard and seen in the world of birds over more than three decades. Known as 'episodic' memory, it stirs recollections that are inextricably merged with a personal experience, embracing three of the five Ws of journalism: 'what, where and when' (who and why being the other two). If I dial up in my head a particular location, it is redolent of the birds I encountered, their images, eccentricities and behaviour all engraved in my memory. Placenames have the power to instantly conjure up a bird for me, while evoking the *genius loci*. Every wing flap or curving flight does not necessarily tell a story, but there are surprising secrets in the winged world. My curiosity and passion were ignited with the skills of identification I learned in Montalto, which was vital to my 'training'. It brought a realisation that most birdwatching is done with your ears, but also led to an understanding that the origins of their names are as fascinating as the birds themselves. I joined nature groups, went off on weekend trips, and built birdwatching into holidays exploring parts of Britain, Europe, Asia and the US, but my binoculars remained firmly fixated on Ireland. The following account of my Irish birding exploits is by no means a complete list. I have merely scratched the surface, but this roll-call reminiscence has sprinkled avian gold dust into my life.

THE NORTH COAST

Wind-blasted, salted and drenched with water twice a day, coastal habitats offer a different birding perspective to forest birds, since they are usually in the water, populating sea stacks and cliffs, or in the air over the sea. At the far northern extremity, off the north Antrim coast, twenty-five shags greeted the arrival of the *Spirit of Rathlin* on its forty-minute journey across the Sea of Moyle from Ballycastle. Four gannets soared in a flypast across the bow, while a bunch of eider ducks bobbed on the waves. As the boat docked in Church Bay, this welcome to the L-shaped Rathlin Island captured the spirit of an internationally important wildlife sanctuary.

People are drawn to the quietude and slow pace of Rathlin life, but for those who visit 'Seabird city', the bird-smothered cliff faces at the west lighthouse, a chaotic marine crossroads, it is far from serene. The tumbling, wheeling and deafening aerial tumult, referred to by Victorian naturalists as 'whirring multitudes', is a barrage of noise and an assault on the senses. Thousands of birds scream and screech with acrobatic twists and turns, crisscrossing above the water, some shooting like white arrows, while others wheel in lazy arcs.

The 'big five' colonies, where a mixed sociable party of guillemots, razorbills, puffins, fulmars and kittiwakes breed from spring to summer, were producing a strong whiff of ammonia in my nostrils. In 2013 the birds numbered around 145,000, but ten years later, estimates put the collective figure at a quarter of a million. Visitors have an affection for the comical and enigmatic puffins, dubbed 'the clowns of the sea', although ferrets and rats have been causing them problems. Endearing guillemots, which have commandeered and whitewashed the roof of a sea stack, stood on densely packed cliff edges or sat on their eggs, while kittiwakes, with their snowy-white heads, wedged on narrow guano-splattered ledges.

Back on the mainland, and on the north coast shore near Castlerock in County Derry, a flock of more than forty effervescent sanderlings was part of an unforgettable Sunday trip in late winter 1996. These beguiling birds, which are long-distance migrants, are small plump waders. Like amusing mechanical clockwork toys, they engaged in brief sprints along the wrack line of the sandy Downhill beach, which stretches to Magilligan Point. We watched them burrow deep into the sand with their long bills, searching for plankton, then scurry away from an incoming surge, before quickly reversing to follow it back out. On that same outing we witnessed a huge congregation of knots, twisting and weaving as they coalesced in a rippling, swirling blend of what looked like dense smoke. The sight of the knots was a smouldering optical illusion as *Calidris canutus* vanished and reappeared before finally departing against a darkening sky to their high-tide roost.

THE WILD ATLANTIC WAY, COUNTY DONEGAL

Long before the tourism gurus came up with the concept of the Wild Atlantic Way in 2014, my family holidayed in north-west Donegal. In the mid-1960s we bowled along the circular Rosguill peninsula in a Riley Kestrel, along what was called 'The Atlantic

Drive'. While we may have been leading a life of Riley in those days, there was little if any interest in the creatures of the air – even though our car boasted a bird-association name. Gulls were viewed as nasty dive-bombers, while oystercatchers ran along the popular beach at Downings; using binoculars was seen as eccentric and the names of birds were unknown to us.

More than five decades later, the 1,500-mile Wild Atlantic Way, voiced by shorebirds, wind and *ceol na mara* – the music of the sea – quickly became a game-changer. In 2014 and for part of 2015, I travelled the length of the coast, training my binoculars on the waves, the water's edge and beaches, which brought me close to many creatures. I was retracing my footsteps from a thirty-day widdershins (anti-clockwise) hitchhiking journey around the coastline in June 1991, which resulted in my first published book: *Irish Shores: A Journey Round the Rim of Ireland*.

On that odyssey, as I stood by the side of roads and next to gardens of houses – sometimes for hours on end while waiting for a lift – my companions were a range of common road runners and road hoppers. They included fidgeting and flapping magpies (a contender for the least-loved bird), hooded crows, pigeons, blackbirds and pied wagtails, all running about like exuberant schoolchildren and rising in a burst of sound. Rock pipits, with their mottled tail feathers and dark legs, were regular coastal sightings, releasing an explosive 'phist' piercing through the wind. Wagtails constantly searched stone walls where red valerian bloomed, looking for insects and spiders' eggs, while from their perch on the top of gorse bushes the bewitching presence of stonechats launched into repeated, high-pitched *weet-tsack-tsack* calls. Even though it was summer, it was bitingly cold; a particularly distressed robin – its throat trembling with the chill – shivered in a way that I mimicked to encourage drivers to pick me up.

As part of the breeding season, the male corncrake was in full voice in the dead of night. Its distinctive call kept me awake in a B&B on the Horn Head Road, near Dunfanaghy. Although I did not see the bird, the nocturnal rasping *crex-crex*-ing call, overlapping with the Atlantic swell coming through the open window, flooded my brain with memories. It was almost dark when I looked out, but all I could see was a vague image of a donkey pricking its ears. A few nights earlier the bird had arrived from its winter quarters in southern Africa.

In the 1980s the corncrake was deeply ingrained within Donegal landscapes, and as the voice of an Irish summer, the bird was heard in many areas around Dunfanaghy and on Tory Island. But by 1988 the total number recorded throughout Ireland was less than 1,000, and by 1991 a campaign was underway to save it. The bird depended on the availability of long vegetation for cover, and farmers were asked to take measures to give it a chance of survival. The usual practice of cutting the fields from the edge towards the middle could trap the broods in long grass with no escape. In many cases, farmers started working in fields protecting the birds by using a 'corncrake friendly' practice. This involved cutting slowly from one side to the other in strips. The birds would then run from the machinery into the safety of a hedge or adjoining field. Fast-forward to the early 2020s, which have seen an increase in the corncrake population, especially in the midlands and County Mayo. Government schemes have encouraged farmers to develop new working methods and the number of recorded corncrake territories stands at the highest figure since the late 1990s.

During several winter visits to Donegal in 2015, I swanned around the Inishowen peninsula, known as the 'Holy Grail' for birdwatchers, as the wildlife wonders rank among the best in Ireland. In a field near the most northerly point at Malin Head my arrival along a mucky lane coincided with a burst of cackling fieldfares, which appeared as though they had just dropped out of the sky on a visit from Scandinavia. A jittery mob, they were busily searching for beetles and earthworms. When they scattered with their *chack-chack* mantra, I noticed their backs were a rich chestnut as they moved into tall trees and hedges. Later that same day, my attention was diverted by the nasal *crronk* of large skeins of Brent geese, which had swept into a field at the far end of Ballyhillin raised beach. A 200-strong flock found its bearings before rising, heading out to sea, circling around, swinging back and settling in another field, wings gleaming and flashing in the sharp light. They rested contentedly before lifting off again with mass cries, until they were lost from view. It had been an exhilarating few days of natural theatre-in-the-wild.

On a low flypast at Inch Levels, a gangly flotilla of whooper swans took off westward, quicksilver white in the autumnal light, wings beating vigorously, a symphonic honking chorus line over my head. The air pulsated and my ears rang with their sonorous, bugle-like calls echoing across the landscape. Tourism bodies refer to the length of time that holiday-makers spend in one area as 'dwell time'. While most visitors stay only a few days in this part of north Donegal, the 'dwell time' of *Cygnus cygnus* extends up to four months. A local farmer I spoke to referred to them as 'clumsy big brutes', but the swans possess a powerful mythological symbolism because they are comfortable in the three habitats of water, land

and air. Their love for the culinary offerings of cereals and crops, and the wet grassland that furnishes a safe roost, combines with the invigorating climate to make a recipe for whooper happiness: nature graced by raw beauty, a symbol of freedom and wildness as they disappear into the horizon.

COUNTY MAYO

Some rivers announce themselves grandly, others trickle along un-obtrusively, but two in Mayo have been blissful hunting grounds for me – not for the gleaming salmon that the area is famed for, but because they are inextricably linked to tail-wagging birds. Palmer-stown Bridge, a long, narrow eighteenth-century masonry bridge, spans the crystal-clear Cloonaghmore river, two miles north of Killala. In 1798, just ten years after its construction, the bridge was used by General Humbert and his French army, who landed at nearby Kilcummin to support the Irish uprising. It was here I stopped the car after the ponderous flight of a heron caught my attention; when scanning the river, I was rewarded with the sight of a pair of grey wagtails, *Motacilla cinerea*, also known as 'water' wagtails. Despite their dull name, they are one of the brightest and nimblest of river birds, but one I had not seen close up, and their grey backs make the yellow of their breasts particularly vivid. The wagtail name is derived from their characteristic habit of continu-ously bobbing or wagging their long slender tail for several min-utes with no sign of exhaustion. From the bridge I observed them making balletic leaps before enhancing their diet with midge lar-vae, small fish, dungflies and worms. The bird's Irish name, *Glasóg liath*, translates as the 'grey-ish-green little thing', and if they are seen near a house, it is a sign that bad news is on the way.

Farther south in Mayo, along the remote Doolough Road, the Erriff is a helter-skelter river flowing near the thunderously cascading Aasleagh Falls, passing under Aasleagh Bridge, unspooling into the fjord at Killary and on to the Atlantic. It was here for the first time that I was transfixed by eye-catching white-throated dippers, spending part of an idyllic afternoon watching their antics, a magical interruption to my journey. Dippers are dumpy and tuxedo-clad. Their Latin name, *Cinclus cinclus*, comes from the ancient Greek for 'tail-wagging', while other names for them are 'river blackbird' and 'little Peggy dishwasher'. In Mayo, the dipper used to be called the 'water crake' and is sometimes still referred to as the 'wee water hen'.

The birds, which have waterproof plumage, live beside spate rivers and can be hard to see, but once I got my eye in, I had a clear view of two adults and a juvenile. When the barrel-chested male came up for air, he blinked and bobbed simultaneously on a wet boulder. With his bright white bib, I could see him fish the river with his eyes for aquatic larvae or crustacea, descending several metres in a quest for food. On a mission towards the bridge, the bird flew low across the water with fast-beating wings, defying the current and jinking with a meandering trajectory, plunging in, resurfacing and returning triumphantly to the same rock with caddisfly and mayfly in his beak. Another two then emerged and briefly submerged before coming up again for air. The currents help push their bodies downward just as the airflow gives them a lift when flying, while their strong claws anchor them to the river bottom. It was an arrestingly beautiful moment and a reminder of the unbridled delight of birdwatching.

Along a narrow coastal road and over a cattle grid at Down-patrick Head on the north Mayo coast, a necklace of breakers was curling in, foaming across wave-eroded slate-grey rocks. Three intimidating stiff-winged fulmars circled the airspace, riding the thermals effortlessly, gliding, banking and following each other. I peered down the dizzyingly steep drop of hundreds of metres, wary of being too close to the fulmars, part of the tube-nosed seabird family, who do not like being disturbed. With acrobatic twists and turns, converging and bisecting, hundreds of yabbering seabirds flew sorties, soaring over my head in tumbling aerial turmoil to their nests on the fifty-metre-high flat-topped Dún Briste sea stack, now a Wild Atlantic Way signature point.

Directly across from me, colonies of kittiwakes were wedged on a staircase of perilously narrow cliff ledges. Shunning the company of the crowd, they pecked each other in a touching cliff-hugging courtship display. On my return walk along the coast, growling and bad-tempered fulmars with stiffly extended wings were riding the thermals. Known as 'ocean wandering nomads', they regarded me as a threat, perhaps to their nest, spitting out repulsive stomach oil at me. 'Fulmar' is a combination of the Old Norse 'ful' and 'mar', meaning 'foul gull', so I increased my pace to a brisk running style, aware of the old adage about discretion being the better part of experiencing a vomiting bird.

Generally, birdwatching is far from a risky pastime, and twenty-five miles west, in the northern half of the Mullet peninsula, a more easy-going party of twites was in full flight. On what was a cold winter's day, about thirty of these small finches were active in fields around Clooneen on the road towards Erris Head. The birds have a characterless look but are rare, and this was a first sighting for me. In nearby fields to the west, a skein of 200 barnacle geese had just arrived from the nearby Inishkea Islands and was grazing on vegetation, enjoying a late breakfast of leaves, roots and stems.

ACHILL ISLAND

In February 2006 I was privileged to be accepted for a two-week residential creative writing stay at the Heinrich Böll cottage at Dugort on Achill Island. This gave me the opportunity to explore the local avifauna by bicycle, as well as reading Böll's *Irish Journal* (1957). The roads around Achill bristle with birdsong and there is a timeless quality to the landscape, while the skyscape is filled with raggedy rainbows. However, it was on the island's pristine beaches of Keel, and in particular Barnyagappul Strand on the other side of Dugort, that I first heard the plaintive whistle of waders moving inland. Beside the silver strand, golden plovers foraged in a huddle for inland earthworms in the goalmouth at either end of a football pitch, tussling around the penalty spot. The small, brightly patterned plovers walked slowly across the grass; they are picky eaters. They employ a stop-run method of feeding, characterised by regular pauses while they scan for food, then dip their bills. In a sudden piece of goalmouth action, one ran to a grassy hump and dipped in a thick orange bill with a black tip, while another quickly joined in. Nearby, dunlin, a sandpiper species, probed the ground and I considered their contrasting strategies of searching for invertebrates. Beyond the pitch, at the tide's edge, oystercatchers were all heads down, tail feathers up, concentrating on the job in hand. They prodded their long orange bills, hammering them in like a pneumatic drill for a few seconds, then continued working the ground in a circle.

THE ARAN ISLANDS

For a few brief moments we were flying in the sky together; seated to my left was the pilot, while to my right through the window was a great black-backed gull. We were en route – two of us in an Aer Arann nine-seater Islander plane – to the Aran Islands off the coast of County Galway. On the flight, the passengers and luggage were weighed so the load could be evenly distributed across the plane, resulting in my front viewing 'sweet spot' seat beside the pilot. The shimmering dazzle of the sea was the same panorama seen by Ireland's largest gull, referred to as 'King of the Atlantic', shuddering in the wind. Mutually, we shared the joint vista across the calm ocean and wide blue skies, to the three islands of Inishmore, Inisheer and Inishmaan, where fishing boats dotted the water. In those few moments, I basked in the sight of *Larus marinus*, absorbing the mighty scale of its enormous jet-black wingspan, powerful beak, snow-white head, pink legs and heavy yellow bill, as well as its aerodynamics of elegance and the forces sustaining flight. I mulled over how birds – long before the days of aircraft – represented the embodiment of flight, and felt seagull-empathy, as well as envy, before being brought back down to earth with a bump on the short runway at the airfield near Killeany. Envy stemmed from the fact that these oceanic birds, which love islands, enjoy this commanding view day in, day out, without any flight phobia, but with the action of air flow on the wing.

While on Inishmore, I saw it only once, but that was enough to recognise it. My attention was caught by the harsh, nasal *tchweek-tchweek* call of a linnet from a drystone wall, followed by its trilling flight notes. Although it may not win an award for being the most striking of birds, the linnet, which breeds on the island, has charisma. For a few minutes, I had the good fortune of capturing through binoculars its short stocky bill as it sat on the limestone pavement, giving me a thrilling view of its chestnut brown back, streaked belly, grey head and splash of crimson on its breast and crown. For days I cycled around the island, and on another stretch of coastline, at Scalpadda, I came across the full stereo of herring, common and black-headed gulls, meadow pipits, rock pipits, dunnock and collared doves.

THE BURREN

The early morning winter light was the colour of dirty concrete, but out to sea a great northern diver was relishing the steely-grey water. My elevated coastal position from the top of a 400-year-old tower on the Burren coast of Clare gave me a view of the rare diver – known in the US as a loon. It was a bird I had long wanted to see, having failed to pin it down on two trips to New England. On the Irish birding grapevine, I had heard that the diver haunted one of my favourite coastal places, Gleninagh, attracted by abundant fish and crab stocks. As I focused my binoculars, a clear view emerged of its dagger-like bill, its sleek body and plumage, which includes a broad black head, thick dark neck with a greenish-blue sheen and an off-white lower face. Now it presented itself before me, riding the waves unconcernedly and bobbing up, performing exercises before skimming along on its belly, showing off its adroit diving manoeuvres.

Of all the locations in Ireland, the Burren offers one of the most outstanding birding experiences because of its diverse terrain. The area is made up of limestone pavement, open scrub, rough upland pasture and woodland, coastal habitats and turloughs which are disappearing lakes found in *poljes*. Over the course of five years, the area became my 'spiritual' home for wildlife.

The Burren is the headquarters of multifarious birds, but above all it is the citadel of the cuckoo. In early May 2009 my first ever sighting of a cuckoo greeted me with an acclamation of arrival in the back garden in Berneens, where I had rented a cottage. These birds make an appearance in the Burren around the end of April or early May, having come all the way from the Congo in West Africa. I was surprised at their size because I had imagined them to be smaller, and they resemble sparrowhawks – but there was no mistake when the bird opened its beak.

On a separate trip, I heard no fewer than five cuckoos booming their woodwind diphone call while I was riding a gypsy cob called Guinness – because he had a black-and-white ear and is good for you. I was on a remote stretch of the Burren Way, south of Ballyvaughan, along single tracks referred to as 'dual cabbage ways'. At the dawn chorus near Lough Rask on a Sunday morning, a torrent of birdsong greeted our small party. The songsters included willow warblers, with their soft *hoo-eet, hoo-eet* increasing in volume before the fading of a sweet string of descending notes; a trilling redpoll with a distinctive call undulating around the lake; the gate-crashing of gregarious sparrows and the deep, insistent croaking *grukk-grukk-grukk* of a pother of ravens tumbling around in the sky.

County Kerry

While the Burren was hard to leave, I pushed onward to the Kingdom – that is the bird kingdom – of Kerry, where in 2014 nothing prepared me for one of the high-water marks of my birding 'career'. At the north side of Dingle Harbour, near a two-arch stone bridge, the tranquil water was populated mostly by dozing ducks, but a rare bird stood in cerebral aloofness. Shaking with excitement, I steadied the binoculars for my first glimpse of a little egret, dressed in dazzling white plumage with a long neck and dagger-like black bill that is exaggerated in size. For more than five undisturbed minutes and with a quickening pulse, I fixed it in my glasses as it embarked on precision stabs of the water, high-stepping through the shallows. When another egret appeared, they performed an obscure but graceful balletic mating dance in the air for a few moments. Their long legs and bills contrasted with a short tail, while their high arching neck stretched skywards, followed by a quick snap down.

It was one of those hold-your-breath moments, and I pinched myself because I could not believe what I was seeing. However, my encounter was short-lived. A group of walkers emerged from a house with an Irish wolfhound, which meant the birds' circle of tolerance – its distance from danger – had been infiltrated and, at the sight of this immense hound, the photogenic *Egretta garzetta* swiftly exited stage left. These birds are said to symbolise not just luck, but also liberation, wisdom and joy, so it was an especially lucky evening. When I started my travels around the country, egrets were unknown in Ireland, although I was familiar with cattle egrets, having seen them in south-west France sitting on the backs of cows. Little egrets started breeding in Ireland in 1997 and are now found in most coastal counties, as well as inland sites.

At Portmagee, on the Ring of Kerry, my gull empathy from that flight to the Aran Islands waned. Large, screaming silver-backed herring gulls, referred to as BFBs – 'Big feral bastards' – started their opportunistic terrorising of tables, helping themselves to tourists' mussels and chips, striking fear into those dining outdoors. At one table, babies in buggies were shrieking, while several adults also turned into cry-babies. One crazed opportunist raided a food refuse bag, tucking into an 'early bird special' as part of a feeding frenzy. Another eyed my ice-cream cone with evil intent and was about to pounce before I escaped inside.

Portmagee is the departure point for a boat trip to the Skellig Islands, best known for a sixth-century monastic outpost that is now a UNESCO world heritage site, and as a haven for seabirds. The boat trip to the two stark pinnacles eight miles off the coast, on what some call the 'scary ferry', is an adventure in itself. My journey, with eleven other hardy souls, was in 'lumpy' seas, referred to by the boatman as 'lazy waves'. As we circled the smaller island, Little Skellig, thousands of gannets with their brilliant white plumage jostled for precious space on the overcrowded ledges, while others dived into the water from all directions. The seabirds – the largest in the northern hemisphere – are supreme show-offs, plunging like jet-fighters into the ocean at speeds of up to fifty-five miles per hour. Forming one of the biggest gannet colonies in the world, at its peak the population on the smaller island rises to a staggering 30,000. I watched them with their eyes facing forward, giving them an intense expression; with their large dagger-like beaks, they were just as scary as the boat trip. It was a dizzying sight, enhanced by swift Manx shearwaters skimming silently across the sea surface, dipping from side to side on stiff wings with their tips almost touching the water.

When the deep swell calmed, we were dropped off at a tiny cove on Skellig Michael. The monks left the island in the twelfth century, and it is now occupied by gannets and hundreds of bright-billed and red-legged portly charismatic puffins, which walk around our feet posing for photographs. As our small party made its way to the summit, a standout sight was the puffins with sand eels in their colourful bills. Their bills hold the skinny and slender silver fish firmly in place, since they are a vital source of food for them and their chicks and are easy to ingest. The steep thirty-minute zigzag ascent on worn flagstones – The Highway to Heaven – leads to the summit of Skellig Michael with its remarkably preserved stone beehive huts and oratories 1,370 feet above sea level.

COUNTY CORK

During a summer walk along a coastal cliff-top path at Ballycotton in east Cork the obstreperous *kweeaw-kweeaw* twanging of birds gave the impression that they were using a loudhailer. The noise belonged to choughs (pronounced chuffs) which, with glossy black plumage and bright crimson feet and legs, shared the path with me, showing their sociable side. The bird is found in Ireland in single pairs or in colonies along the south and west coasts and islands. With their dark, blue-sheened plumage and distinctive broad wings, they diverted off my path on short nosedives, stabbing their red bills into close-cropped turf searching for insect larvae. A dozen prepared for take-off and, as I observed their acrobatic soaring flight, wheeling and roaring, with their widely separated primary feathers spread out like fingers, I detected a metallic purple and blue sheen. Sometimes referred to as 'personality plus' crows, choughs are members of the crow family and would soon be pairing off to find crevices and cliffs in which to nest and raise young.

INLAND IRELAND AND THE RIVER SHANNON

They are known as Ireland's 'sky-dancers', and I was told that there was only a slender chance of catching sight of them. I set off on an April afternoon in 2002 to climb Slieve Beagh – the highest point in County Monaghan – with hope in my heart. Birdwatchers, I discover, adopt a positive approach, and if they do not find the bird they are seeking, then something else may crop up and they will still have enjoyed the outdoors. In this area, merlin, peregrine falcon, curlew, golden plover and dunlin were known to thrive.

But my scrutiny was on hen harriers, magnificent raptors that nest on Slieve Beagh, according to my intelligence information. I spent several hours tramping across burnt patches of heather and scrub to reach the highest point at Eshnabrack, and on my return the harriers emerged from hiding. It was exhilarating to watch them glide as they hunted for mice, voles and smaller birds, such as skylarks or meadow pipits. With a butterfly-like flight, they circled slowly and deliberately. They have well-designed curved beaks and strong claws to catch and hold on to their prey as they quarter the upland. For several minutes the ghostly grey male and the large brown female conducted an elaborate sky-dancing routine, which is part of the seduction of a courtship ritual. In other parts of Monaghan, they say that the birds 'sing in Latin'; this refers not so much to their scientific names or musical calls, but to the townland of Latton in the parish of Aughnamullen.

The presiding spirit of my River Shannon trip in 2018 was a quest for the bird that had constantly eluded me in Ireland. Ornithology christens it *Alcedo atthis*, but most recognise it by its common name of kingfisher. It is also known in Irish as *biorra an uisce*, meaning 'water-spear'. The only time I had seen one was on a trip to Indonesia, when I rose at 5 a.m. to walk the length of Sanur beach on Bali. When I got there, a dazzling small blue kingfisher was sitting on fishing traps; with the changing colour of the light, its iridescence switched from a brilliant blue to sapphire and then turquoise.

Throughout my Shannon journey I found images of kingfishers on bicycle signs for the Kingfisher Trail, on Indian restaurant beer bottle labels, on B&Bs, on magazine covers and elsewhere, but pinning down the real thing proved much more difficult. Off and on for many months the bird played hide-and-seek with me. My starting point was Cavan, where on my way through fields to the Shannon Pot, I caught sight and sound of a disappearing jack snipe. I heard the bird performing its percussive *tick-tock* drumming ritual in long cover, before rising with a sharp call and skittering away in a sudden flight of panicky zigzags.

In Carrick-on-Shannon, cantankerous moorhens flew on short sorties across the water as I wandered along the boardwalk. Rivalling the squeaky hens, on a night out with pink hats, tight, sequinned dresses, and cowboy boots, was a hen party of fifteen young women.

It was in Carrick that I learned a fascinating snippet of information from a duck specialist who was monitoring populations. He explained that the angle of the wake-lines of a duck moving through the water and forming the arms of a V chevron is always fixed at thirty-nine degrees, irrespective of its speed. The 'Kelvin wake pattern' as it is known was first discovered by Lord Kelvin. Could you, he wondered, go through life without that knowledge?

There are over 130 species of duck worldwide and while their beauty is often in the eye of the beholder, along the Shannon one man in Lanesborough shared his love with me for pintail, mallard, Appleyard, Muscovy and small domestic Call ducks. Every morning and evening, Dan, the duck charmer, follows his *grá* for the ducks by feeding them a generous breakfast. As they paddled around in circles, the ducks quacked, nibbled, pinched and poked one another. The most unusual one among them was the scarce and secretive West Indian whistling duck. A large brown bird with black-and-white speckles, an elongated neck, long legs and big feet, there is an exoticism to the bird which has travelled thousands of miles from its home in the Caribbean wetlands to the Shannon waters. Its loud shrill whistle is reminiscent of a referee ending a football match.

Farther south, while waiting for a boat to take me out on a research visit to the Black Islands on Lough Ree – the largest of the three major Shannon lakes, which sprawls with numerous islands – the air rippled with the symphonic purity of birdsong chatter. The shoreline teemed with birds plummeting, quivering and announcing their presence through calls and songs, wing beats, shaking branches and whistles, a transitory snapshot between water, sky, trees and earth. One by one, in four-and-five-second bursts, robin, blackbird, wren, song thrush, great tit, greenfinch and willow warbler called out a series of clicks, sighs, stutters and plaintive whispers. On the lake, wigeon, curlew, mute swans and waders were holding court, adding to the party atmosphere, while a lone coot busied itself fidgeting in another corner of the bay and a shelduck trailed a crèche of chicks.

On a different boat, a Viking vessel, I arrived in Clonmacnoise from Athlone. Under a bright spring sunlight, passengers were greeted on disembarkation with the bubbling descant of skylarks, known as 'sky-flappers'. For nigh on ten minutes these doughty birds – widely celebrated in poetry and music – performed acrobatic displays, hovering effortlessly, then bouncing up and down as if on a piece of elastic. At the same time they continued their vertiginous but disorganised sprinkling of urgent notes from a dizzying height of more than 100 metres. During spring and summer the birds eschew terra firma, though the ground is where they spend much of the rest of their lives nesting, sleeping and feeding.

Four miles south, at Shannonbridge, groups of sand martins nesting nearby were weaving in and out of the old bridge, a strategic crossing-point on the Shannon linking Roscommon with Offaly dating from 1757. Boisterous and social birds, the martins curved low over the surface of the river, snatching insects on the wing before returning to their burrows to feed their nestlings. The martins are related to swallows and house martins, collectively referred to as hirundines.

Mountshannon, County Clare

Not yet lucky enough to have seen the elusive kingfisher, my next stop was Mountshannon, where I was on a specific mission, to see a much bigger species of rare bird – white-tailed eagles, commonly called 'sea eagles'. The species was persecuted to extinction in Ireland by hunting, poisoning and egg-collecting in the early 1900s, but as part of a reintroduction project, they had been breeding successfully since 2012 on the western side of Lough Derg. The eagles, Saoirse and Caimin, made history when they reared the first chicks to fledge from a nest in Ireland for more than century. They welcomed an addition to their family in spring 2017, which coincided with my visit. Such was the interest that a specially designed Portakabin was set up as an information and viewing point at Mountshannon harbour. The hide was equipped with high-powered telescopes and binoculars trained on a nest in trees in the far distance across the lake at Cribby. Details and photographs of the eagles' status were posted on the walls and there was even a sign in the main street pointing 'This way to the sea eagles.'

By wingspan and weight the white-tailed is the largest eagle in Europe and although I did not witness the male bird in flight, it was nevertheless a spectacular sight through the scope. I unhurriedly appreciated the heft and scale of his upper body and head-turning. Adding to its mystique, the bird was partially camouflaged by the trees, blending in with the colour scheme. When I caught it in sharp focus, the size and glow of his severe-looking, vivid yellow hooked beak with rounded curve was immediately striking. The nature writer Jim Crumley once memorably described the sea eagle's beak as 'a cross between a banana and a machete'. The eagle's manner and pose indicated a certain crankiness, unhappy with his lot, hungry for fish or mammals. The head and neck feathers were a conspicuously pale yellow-brown, and while he was mostly motionless, his fixed gaze was alert for any nourishment opportunities that may present themselves.

The presence of the bird was causing a stir in the cabin, and while most other eagle-watchers were quiet, one or two shared tips and feelings. 'It's just breathtaking,' said one woman, while another woman shivered and said that seeing him gave her the 'heebie-jeebies'. Back at the scope, I noted the pale yellow of the bird's eye – a single defining image. The afterglow impression was of an otherworldly raptor, almost medieval and most definitely a creature with which I would not like to tussle. Its Gaelic name, *Iolaire suile na greine*, means 'the eagle with the sunlit eye' and, unquestionably, it was the most magnificent bird's-eye view of a bird's eye that I have ever experienced.

From Mountshannon my journey took me south to Limerick, where peculiar one-legged wonders along the quaysides transfixed me. Several leggy grey herons – Ireland's largest predatory wading bird and as motionless as a marble statue – stood with necks stretched out at O'Callaghan's Strand, although their stance was startlingly only on one leg. A short distance from them, three graceful-looking black-headed gulls perched on one leg, while the other leg was tucked up underneath their body to keep warm. This is to help reduce the amount of skin that is exposed and may reflect the chilly Limerick climate. On railings farther along, more than thirty black-headed gulls lined up as though at a beauty parade, eyes fixed on the river, but holding to the principle of safety in numbers – and, in their case, two legs.

In early afternoon, at Custom House Quay in Limerick, I boarded *The Eye of the River* for a boat trip with Pat Lysaght. We were on the Abbey River heading north to Corbally where birdlife is scarce. Along the way, placenames tripped off his tongue with casual familiarity: Clancy's Quay, Curragower Falls, Thomond Weir, Parteen, Ardnacrusha. Without warning, after thirty minutes a bird came arrowing, low and fast, along the river, a streak of electric, laser-bright blue. Through binoculars, I glimpsed its dagger bill and bright stripe, a flying furnace of magical colour. As it shot past, dead straight, wingbeats whirring, the bird winked at me – perhaps for luck, a reward for patience. The kingfisher sighting was not a surprise to Pat, who was used to seeing them washing and cleaning themselves along sections of the waterway. 'They're just birds after all, aren't they?' he exclaimed. That may be so, but for me this sighting held a sense of occasion, an example of perseverance paying off and heeding the advice I had received from an ornithologist: 'Let the bird find you.'

THE EAST COAST

The east coast of Ireland is far from a foreign country for birds but my internal compass mostly pointed to the magical realm of the west as my preferred direction. However, during a chilly January 2002 trip in the south-east, I witnessed an assemblage of thousands of wintering waterbirds at the natural haven of Wexford Harbour with its sandbars and mudbanks. The harbour is the lower part of the River Slaney estuary, conjoined with flat areas of farmland, with the unappealing-sounding name Wexford Slobs; they are wild salt marshes.

Late one afternoon, with birds zooming around in every direction, the scale of numbers and the noise of the wingbeats presented an awesome problem in terms of focusing, never mind counting. Twilight was approaching and the water was aswarm with waders. Amongst a confused babble of voices and kinetic energy, I identified twenty species of wintering waterbirds. Dunlin followed the shoreline while bar-tailed godwits, with a hunched look, and redshanks were in a face-off over their shared space. In another area, Bewick's, mute and whooper swans were feeding, preening and loafing, before embarking on angry charges of activity across the water. A variety of gulls and terns looked suitably unimpressed with the goings-on. Ducks, including red-breasted merganser, shoveler, pochard and pintail, were dabbling, while Brent geese were gabbling. There was a settled feel to the birding ambience that said, 'I may be here for some time.' It was an astonishing spectacle which washed over me as darkness closed in. The haunting call of white-fronted geese from Greenland – colloquially known in Ireland as 'bog geese' – cut through the air. I departed in the dark to the ear-splitting two-note piping *whee-oooo, whee-oooo* whistles of a flight of wigeon.

Farther north along the east coast, the distinctive, long, rasping *raaak, raaak* call, as well as a gentler *chu-ick, chu-ick* was an accompaniment on a boat across the lough from Carlingford in County Louth to Greencastle in County Down. The calls belonged to the delicate roseate terns, recently arrived in June from their West African wintering grounds and one of the highlights on my hitchhiking journey around Ireland. In the 1970s there was a large colony of them in the lough with up to 600 pairs. When I was there in the early 1990s the numbers had seriously decreased, but they had begun to stabilise and to breed again successfully on eastern coastal counties. On a sweep across the lough with a local pilot and fisherman, Peadar Elmore, on his boat the *Queen Maeve*, we came across the exquisite birds with their black bill and a hint of red. A small committee of terns was perched on shingle at Green Island, showing off their red legs and long tail streamers. We also sailed past a gulp of six funereal cormorants, wings akimbo in a drip-dry position, perched on waterside foliage, all facing different directions. Large, black and conspicuous, with reptilian necks, the cormorants have a prehistoric appearance and weary expressions of resignation.

On the northern side of Carlingford Lough, the Mourne Mountains stretch across south Down. While hiking there I have come across the wheatear, a bird beloved of the upland. Part of the wheatear's *raison d'être* is bouncing at speed over boulders, disappearing into the distance, and you have to be alert to spot it. Since the bird is a migrant visitor, it is seen only in the spring or summer. My sightings have been near Cove Mountain and on the approach to the granite tors of Slieve Bearnagh – another stronghold of the bird is at Black Head and Fanore in County Clare. The wheatear is one of the most gloriously named of all birds: because of its distinctive white rump and the fact that the origins of its name are Anglo-Saxon – coming from 'hvit' meaning 'white' and 'aerse' – it is known under the moniker 'white-arse'.

STRANGFORD LOUGH

With its long, thin wispy plume, the stocky bird that captured my attention on Strangford Lough was a lone lapwing. The bird likes to draw attention to itself with its evocative *pee-wit-pee-wit* rising in pitch on the second note. Its colours came into sharp focus from the white neck, dark bill and purple feathers, down to long pink legs, but it was not entirely friendless. Soon the bird was joined by another dozen, mucking around mudflats along parts of the coast between Mount Stewart and Greyabbey, and searching for wireworms and leatherjackets. They engaged in a start-stop feeding routine, then snaffled invertebrates and insects. With a short run, they took off in wavering flight, interspersed with tumbles and twists, before hanging in the sky for a brief moment. Within thirty minutes of my visit, at least 200 had gathered at different points along the shorefront, where more than 2,000 lapwings arrive for the winter. A flock of them, known as a deceit, is one of the more uncomplimentary collective nouns in birding lingua franca, but for all that they are referred to as 'the national bird of Ireland'.

Farther around the lough shore ringed plovers were active. They are delightfully dumpy, short-legged wading birds with brownish grey and white colouring. The birds, which drill in the sand with their large downturned bills and orange legs, are known in this part of County Down as 'sand trippers', as distinct from the day-trippers who also frequent the beaches.

The Castle Espie Wetland Centre, on the western shore of Strangford Lough, is the destination for an array of birds in a mosaic of habitats providing foraging grounds. The castle that gave the reserve its name no longer exists, but its nickname, Castle 'Eye-spy', persists with birdwatchers. On a July day a screaming party unfolded, with slender common terns in a fluster as they flew over a pontoon, bringing food and protecting their young with anxious squeals. With orange-red beaks and a black tip, the terns perched on wooden posts while others flew in and out. The adults made regular trips back to the pontoon, but it was far from a case of 'many happy re-terns'. As a tranquil contrast, in another part of the wetlands, oblivious to the nearby airborne drama, more than 500 oystercatchers sunbathed as part of a shingle siesta. Most lay stretched out with their orange beaks visible, while a small number stood or paddled at the water's edge.

BELFAST

It was just before sunset on a calm evening in mid-November and I had alighted from my bike at the Albert Bridge along the River Lagan in Belfast to see one of the most spectacularly rewarding birding experiences – starlings gathering in their thousands in the early evening sky, turning it black as part of their murmuration. Along with a small group of passers-by, I watched in awe as the birds moved with precision and speed, wondering how they managed to avoid colliding with one another. Sudden changes of direction and pace were part of a free shapeshifting show, which would be running each day from then until the spring. There was a primeval feel to this mesmerising performance as the birds rose, plummeted and drifted apart in a dark cloud, then cut and dived in many directions. Were they exchanging information, confusing predators, indulging in a formation flying party? Like so much in the world of birding, we may never know the correct answer.

Glossary

Amber list	Bird species that are of medium conservation concern
Apricity	Warmth of the winter sun
Arboreal	Living in the trees, above ground
Ash dieback	A fungal disease of ash trees
Biodiversity	Biological diversity, referring to the different types of living organisms in a given area
Breeding grounds	Broad term for the geographical range of birds over which a species normally breeds
Call	Any bird vocalisation that is not a song
Canopy	Continuous network of branches and foliage forming the top vertical layer in a forest
Corvids	Members of the crow family
Crown shyness	The border around trees where they desist from getting too close to touching one another
Drumming	Sound made by the beating of a woodpecker's bill for the purpose of proclaiming its presence
Fasciation	A mutation resulting in extra flowerheads which can also affect stems
Fledgling	A bird that has fledged and left the nest
Flight-song	A song that is delivered as an accompaniment to a display flight
Frond	Leaf of a fern, comprising frond blade and stalk
Genius loci	Prevailing spirit of a place

Gestalt	Shape of a pattern or configuration of wording
Hirundines	Collective name for swallows and sand and house martins
Hoodies	Local term for hooded crows
Indented leaves	Strongly toothed leaves
Jizz	Term for overall impression of birds
Lammas growth	Occurs in buds and branches in early August
Leaf litter	Layer of undecayed plant material on the woodland floor
Littoral	Living by the shore of the sea or a lake
Locus amoenus	Pleasant place
Migrant	A bird species that migrates, often over long distances
Moulting	The act of birds replacing worn-out feathers
Ovate leaf	Egg-shaped leaf which is broadest near the base
Passerine	Perching bird
Petrichor	The smell of the earth after rain
Polje	Flat-floored depression within karst limestone, found in the Burren, County Clare
Post-pluvial	Coming after rain
Probing	Searching for food below a surface such as grass or mud
Quartering	Birds flying slowly and low above ground, searching for food below
Red list	Birds that are globally threatened and of high conservation concern
Resident	Birds that remain all year in the same area
Root ball	Trees planted with a compact mass of roots which allow new growth

Rugose   Leaves that are rough and wrinkled

Saproxylic   Organism living in a decaying wood

Shifting baseline syndrome   A type of change to how a system is measured, against previous reference points

Skulking   Customarily remaining hidden low in thick vegetation

Sky-dancing   Elaborate display flight, mostly refers to hen harriers

Song-flight   Birds' aerial routine for advertising purposes accompanied by a song

Stop-run-peck feeding   Method of feeding by sight, notably used for the plover family

Syrinx   The sound-producing apparatus of birds, located at the base of the windpipe

Thinning out   Removal of a few trees every five to ten years

Tube-nosed   Seabirds of the family *Procellariidae*, mostly fulmars and petrels

Vernalisation   Winter process of speeding the flowering of plants

Veteran tree   Usually (but not necessarily) a very old tree with significant cultural, biological or aesthetic value – sometimes all three

Whorled leaves   Three or more leaves arising from a stem at the same point

Wind flotsam   The bits and pieces caught in tree roots that have formed a type of net, catching anything

Woodies   Term for wood pigeons

Select Bibliography

Armstrong, D. and Simms, M.J., *The Heart of Down: Paintings and Stories from the Countryside, Villages and Towns of Mid-Down* (Donaghadee: Cottage Publications, 2000).

Bardon, J., *A History of Ulster* (Belfast: Blackstaff Press, 1992).

— *A History of Ireland in 250 Episodes* (Dublin: Gill & Macmillan, 2008).

Bence-Jones, M., *A Guide to Irish Country Houses* (London: Constable, 1988).

Bew, J., *Castlereagh: Enlightenment, War and Tyranny* (Oxford: Oxford University Press, 2011).

Brett, C., *Historic Buildings, Groups of Buildings, Areas of Architectural Importance in the Towns and Villages of Mid Down* (Belfast: Ulster Architectural Heritage Society, 1974).

Carr, P., *Portavo, An Irish Townland and its Peoples. Part One: Earliest Times to 1844* (Belfast: White Row Press, 2003).

— *Portavo, An Irish Townland and its Peoples. Part Two: The Famine to the Present* (Belfast: White Row Press, 2005).

Dawson, K.L., *The Belfast Jacobin: Samuel Neilson, and the United Irishmen* (Dublin: Irish Academic Press, 2017).

Dickson, C., *Revolt in the North: Antrim and Down in 1798* (London: Constable, 1997).

Dooley, T. and Ridgway, C. (eds), *The Intellectual World of the Country House in Ireland and Britain* (Dublin: Four Courts Press, 2024).

Evans, E.E., *Mourne Country* (Dundalk: Dundalgan Press, 1951).

Fennell, A., *Heritage Trees of Ireland* (Cork: Collins Press, 2013).

Gibney, J. (ed.), *The United Irishmen, Rebellion and the Act of Union, 1798–1803* (Barnsley: Pen & Sword, 2018).

Harris, W., *The Antient and Present State of the County of Down, 1744* (Ballynahinch: Davidson Books reprint, 1977).

Hill, M., Turner, B. and Dawson, K. (eds), *1798: Rebellion in County Down* (Newtownards: Colourpoint, 1998).

Johnston, J.M., *Heterogenea or Medley for the Benefit of the Poor* (Downpatrick: James Parks, 1803).

Kenny, M., *The 1798 Rebellion: Photographs and Memorabilia from the National Museum of Ireland* (Dublin: Town House and Country House, 1996).

Killen, J. (ed.), *The Decade of the United Irishmen, Contemporary Accounts 1791–1801* (Belfast: Blackstaff Press, 1998).

— *The United Irishmen and the Government of Ireland, 1791–1801* (Belfast: Linenhall Library, 1998).

Leslie, R.J. and Sloan, G., *Old Ballynahinch* (Catrine, Ayrshire: Stenlake, 2012).

Lewis, S., *County Down: A Topographical Dictionary of the Parishes, Villages and Towns of County Down in the 1830s* (Belfast: Friar's Bush Press, 2003).

Lyttle, W.G., *Betsy Gray or Hearts of Down: A Tale of Ninety-Eight* (Newcastle: *Mourne Observer*, 1968).

Maguire, W.A. (ed.), *Up in Arms! The 1798 Rebellion in Ireland* (Belfast: Ulster Museum, 1998).

McCarthy, P., *Life in the Country House in Georgian Ireland* (London: Yale University Press, 2016).

McCullough, S., *Ballynahinch, Centre of Down* (Ballynahinch: Chamber of Commerce, 1968).

Nelson, E.C., 'Sir Arthur Rawdon (1662–1695) of Moira: His Life, and Letters, Family and Friends and his Jamaican Plants', *Belfast Natural History and Philosophical Society, 157th–161st Sessions, Proceedings and Reports*, 2nd Series, Vol. 10 (8 December 1981), pp. 30–48.

— *The Wild & Garden Plants of Ireland* (Bicester, Oxfordshire: Coles Books, 2009).

— and Walsh, W.F., *An Irish Flower Garden Replanted: The Histories of Some of Our Garden Plants* (Castlebourke: De Burca, 1997).

O'Byrne, R., *The Irish Aesthete: Buildings of Ireland, Lost and Found* (Dublin: Lilliput Press, 2024).

O'Clery, C., *The Star Man* (Bantry: Somerville Press, 2016).

O'Donnell, R., *1798 Diary* (Dublin: Irish Times Books, 1998).

O'Farrell, P. (ed.), *The '98 Reader* (Dublin: Lilliput Press, 1998).

Pakenham, Thomas, *The Year of Liberty: The Great Irish Rebellion of 1798* (London: Abacus, 2000).

Praeger, R.L., *Official Guide: County Down Tourist District, Belfast* (Belfast: Belfast and County Down Railway Company, The Linenhall Press, 1900).

Reid, H., 'Five Montalto Dynasties', *Lecale Review, A Journal of Down History*, Lecale & Downe Historical Society, No. 16 (Downpatrick, 2018), pp. 4–10.

Robinson, K., *North Down and Ards in 1798* (Bangor: North Down Heritage, 1998).

Smith, P., *Buildings of South County Down* (Belfast: Ulster Architectural Heritage Society, 2019).

Somerville-Large, P., *The Irish Country House: A Social History* (London: Sinclair-Stevenson, 1995).

Stack, W., *Rebellion, Invasion and Occupation: The British Army in Ireland, 1793–1815* (Warwick: Helion & Company, 2021).

Stewart, A.T.Q., *The Summer Soldiers: 1798 Rebellion in Antrim and Down* (Belfast: Blackstaff Press, 1995).

Taylor, G. and Skinner, A., *Maps of the Roads of Ireland* (London: G. Nicol, 1777).

Webb, R.M., *The John Hogg Group, 1890–1990: The First Hundred Years* (marketing material, Advertising Artists, 1990).

Wilsdon, B., *The Sites of the 1798 Rising in Antrim and Down* (Belfast: Blackstaff Press, 1997).

Acknowledgements

No book is written alone and many individuals responded to my enquiries while others offered encouragement and inspiration. At Montalto estate, the owner Gordon Wilson provided thoughtful suggestions; the head gardener Lesley Heron and forester John Gardiner were supportive in fact-finding during my tours of the rejuvenated grounds and I benefited from their discussions. In the publicity office, Victoria Ward and Jason McCusker supplied photographs, contacts and general information, and I am grateful to them.

The writers and historians, Peter Carr, Kenneth Dawson and Horace Reid were of considerable help in checking historical accuracy. They have extensive knowledge of Montalto and its past, and Horace has produced videos dealing with the history of the estate, which are on YouTube. For their time and generosity of spirit I would like to thank Francis McLean, Andrew Carlisle, the former Montalto gamekeeper Ian Jamison and wildlife expert Wilson Johnston.

At the indispensable Heritage Library in Downpatrick, Briege Stitt is a fount of knowledge on mid-Down and I am indebted to her for the help she gave me by digging deep into local history files and books. I appreciate the assistance of Ciaran Toal at Lisburn Museum and would like to record my thanks to the staff at Ballynahinch Library, as well as the Linen Hall Library and Central Library in Belfast, who located out-of-print books.

The photographer, cameraman and filmmaker Trevor Ferris

once again collaborated with me on this book. He worked his magic with images, offering imaginative suggestions with photographs and drone footage, and I am grateful to him for his skills and knowledge.

Síne Quinn, commissioning editor at Merrion Press, first triggered the idea of looking back at life in Montalto in the early 1990s. She played a crucial part in moving this project – which might be described as 'intergenerational collaboration' – towards publication. Thanks to her and to Conor Graham, as well as senior editor Wendy Logue for her blend of finesse and perception; copy editor Heidi Houlihan, who ensured uniformity across the manuscript; publicist Ciara Kinsella; cover designer Karen Vaughan; and the rest of the editorial team for their scrupulous work and kindness.

I would like to thank Jacquie Moore for permission from the Office of the President to reproduce 'The Battle of Ballynahinch' by Thomas Robinson.

Excerpts from Ted Hughes' 'Deceptions,' 'Spring Nature Notes,' and 'Trees' are reprinted from *Collected Poems*, edited by Paul Keegan, Faber, 2003, and are reproduced by permission of Faber and Faber Ltd. The excerpt from 'Like Snow' by Robert Graves, *The Complete Poems in One Volume*, edited by Beryl Graves and Dunstan Ward, 2000, is reprinted by permission of Carcanet Press UK. The lines from Patrick Kavanagh's 'Spraying the Potatoes' are reprinted from *Collected Poems*, edited by Antoinette Quinn, Allen Lane, 2004, by kind permission of the Trustees of the Estate of the late Katherine B. Kavanagh, through the Jonathan Williams Literary Agency.

Every effort has been made to contact copyright-holders prior to publication. In some instances this has proved difficult. If notified, the publisher will be pleased to rectify any omission at the earliest opportunity.

For their interest and suggestions, I value the support of Terence Bowman, Rose Cremin, Carole Davidson, Michael Fewer, Jack Johnston, Claire Jones, Mary Kelly, Noel McAdam, Chris Murphy, Patricia Pyne, Emma Smith, Peter Somersett, Charlie Warmington and Paul Wilson.

With his wise counsel, my literary agent Jonathan Williams has consistently encouraged me by reading the proofs, and I am indebted to him for his astute advice and guidance not just for this book but over the past two decades.

A heartfelt thank-you to my wife Felicity, who has broken into print with her contribution, and to our son Daniel for their continued and unfailing support. They have been of inestimable help with research, reading drafts and assisting with technical issues. Any mistakes or inaccuracies are mine.

To all those custodians of the countryside and landscape who work hard to restore and protect Ireland's unique habitats and wildlife, I salute you; to those suffering eco-anxiety, please listen and support each other's well-being. Encourage a friend to become a 'wild-lifer', to engage with the restorative power of nature, to celebrate it, and to care for the precious ecosystem as never before. In the words of the Chinese proverb: 'It is always better to light a candle than to curse the darkness.'

Paul Clements,
April 2025

Index

By the Same Author

Bookshops of Belfast
Irish Shores: A Journey Round the Rim of Ireland
Jan Morris: A Critical Study
The Height of Nonsense: The Ultimate Irish Road Trip
Burren Country: Travels Through an Irish Limestone Landscape
Romancing Ireland: Richard Hayward, 1892–1964, A Biography
A Walk Through Carrick-on-Shannon, Co. Leitrim
Wandering Ireland's Wild Atlantic Way: From Banba's Crown
to World's End
An Enduring Investment Thread: A History of Cunningham Coates
Shannon Country: A River Journey Through Time
Jan Morris: Life from Both Sides, A Biography

As Editor

The Blue Sky Bends Over All: A Celebration of Ten Years of the
Immrama Festival of Travel Writing
Jan Morris: Around the World in Eighty Years, A Tribute
Legacy: A Collection of Personal Testimonies from People Affected by the
Troubles in Northern Ireland

As Contributing Writer

In a Harbour Green: Celebrating Benedict Kiely
Westward Ho! A Ramble Through Galway, 1840–1950: Collected Essays
A Benedict Kiely Reader: Drink to the Bird and Selected Essays
Fodor's Ireland
Insight Guide Belfast
Insight Guide Ireland
Rough Guide to Ireland